CONTEMPORARY'S

GED

TEST 3: SCIENCE

EXERCISE BOOK

CB
CONTEMPORARY
BOOKS
CHICAGO

Writer
Robert Mitchell

Published by Contemporary Books, Inc.
Two Prudential Plaza, Chicago, Illinois 60601-6790
Manufactured in the United States of America
International Standard Book Number: 0-8092-4598-1
10 9 8 7 6 5 4 3 2 1

Published simultaneously in Canada by
Fitzhenry & Whiteside
195 Allstate Parkway
Markham, Ontario L3R 4T8
Canada

Contents

Acknowledgments

Article on page 20 from *Science Digest*, March 1984. Reprinted by permission.

Excerpt on page 26 from "Leeches Make a Comeback" in *Science Digest*, February 1985. Reprinted by permission.

Excerpt on page 61 from "High Blood Pressure: Drugless Treatment?" in *Science Digest*, March 1987. Reprinted by permission.

Article on page 62 from *Science Digest*, May 1986. Reprinted by permission.

Article on page 74 from *Science Digest*, August 1984. Reprinted by permission.

Article on page 76 from *Science Digest*, February 1985. Reprinted by permission.

The editor has made every effort to trace the ownership of all copyrighted material. Should there prove to be any question regarding the use of any material, regret is here expressed for such error. Upon notification of any such oversight, proper acknowledgment will be made in future editions.

Introduction

Welcome to *Contemporary's GED Science Exercise Book*. It will help you study for the GED Science Test. There are five main sections in this exercise book: Plant and Animal Biology, Human Biology, Earth Science, Chemistry, and Physics. Each section gives you additional practice in an area covered in Contemporary's main science textbook, *GED Test 3: Science*. The organization of this exercise book parallels that of the main science textbook, so if you need a review or further instruction, refer to our main science text.

This exercise book also contains a full-length practice test. This test is very similar to the actual GED Science Test. It's the same length as the GED Test, and it's in the same format.

OVERVIEW OF THE GED SCIENCE TEST

The GED Science Test consists of multiple-choice questions. These questions require you to know some basic science concepts. However, the test emphasizes your ability to think about these concepts. You will not have to recall an isolated fact or date as on some tests. Rather, you will read a passage or look at an illustration and answer questions based on it.

There are 66 multiple-choice questions, and you will be given 95 minutes to complete the test. About two-thirds of the questions will be based on reading passages of up to 250 words each, and one-third will be based on diagrams, charts, or graphs.

CONTENT AREAS

The passages on the GED Science Test are taken from the following content areas:

Content Area	Percentage of Test
Life Sciences Biology	50%
Physical Sciences Earth Science Chemistry Physics	50%

Keep in mind that a given question may draw from more than one of these topics. It's hard to discuss science without touching on a number of topics. For example, a question on air pollution may draw from material covered in both biology and chemistry.

READING SKILLS

The GED Science Test also tests your ability to think about certain ideas and concepts. You will be asked to do more than just find an answer that was given in a passage.

The thinking skills and their respective percentages are:

Reading Skill	Percentage of Test
Comprehension	20%
Application	30%
Analysis	30%
Evaluation	20%

In addition to the reading passages found throughout this exercise book, you will find many visuals such as charts, graphs, and diagrams. These kinds of visuals make up about 30 percent of the test.

At the end of the book is a complete answer key that tells you the reasoning behind each correct answer choice. Be sure to check your answers and read the explanations. This will help you improve your skill in answering multiple-choice questions.

To determine whether or not you are ready to take the real GED Science Test, we recommend that you take the practice test in this book. The evaluation chart that follows the test will help you determine the areas in which you may need additional practice.

At the beginning of each section in this exercise book, you'll see references to *text pages*. These page numbers refer to *Contemporary's GED Test 3: Science*. Go back to the appropriate pages whenever you need a review.

Plant and Animal Biology

Text pages 81–111

Questions 1–5 refer to the following information.

Biologists have discovered that the Earth can be divided into large regions of similar characteristics. Each region, called a *biome*, has a certain type of climate and contains certain dominant plants and animals. The United States is made up of five such biomes:

tundra—The tundra is a region with a very cold, dry climate. Many animals in the tundra are white, so they blend into their snowy surroundings. The small plants that can survive in the tundra are adapted to a growing season of only about sixty days.

coniferous forest—The coniferous forest is known for its cone-bearing trees that stay green all year long. These trees, also known as evergreens, often have thin, needle-like leaves.

deciduous forest—The deciduous forest is known for having a long growing season. Its colorful broad-leafed trees lose their leaves each autumn.

grasslands—Grasslands are mainly found where rainfall is not heavy enough to support large trees. Grasslands provide rich farming and grazing land.

desert—A desert is a very dry area that will support neither tree growth nor extensive grass. In most deserts, rainfall averages less than ten inches each year.

1. In Barrow, Alaska, the average yearly rainfall is less than ten inches. The average temperature in January is 19° F below zero. Home of glaciers and polar bears, this part of Alaska is in the biome known as

   (1) tundra   (4) grasslands
   (2) coniferous forest   (5) desert
   (3) deciduous forest

2. In autumn, the forests of Maine and Vermont change from green to the blazing yellows, oranges, reds, and purples of fall. These trees are part of the biome known as

   (1) tundra   (4) grasslands
   (2) coniferous forest   (5) desert
   (3) deciduous forest

3. The Great Plains of the central United States are famous for the herds of bison that once grazed in those vast open spaces. Now, this same land grows the corn and grain that supplies much of the world's food. The Great Plains are in the biome best identified as

   (1) tundra   (4) grasslands
   (2) coniferous forest   (5) desert
   (3) deciduous forest

4. In order to keep water loss to a minimum, the cholla plant conserves water in its thick stem, and the leaves of the cholla are thin spines. Chollas can withstand very high temperatures. These features enable a cholla plant to survive in which of the following biomes?

   (1) tundra   (4) grasslands
   (2) coniferous forest   (5) desert
   (3) deciduous forest

5. Pine trees grow well in a hot, relatively dry climate while fir trees seem to thrive in a cool, damp climate. However, pine and fir trees are similar in that most species have cones and needle-shaped leaves. These trees are found in the biome known as

   (1) tundra   (4) grasslands
   (2) coniferous forest   (5) desert
   (3) deciduous forest

ANSWERS ARE ON PAGE 82.

Questions 6–10 refer to the information below.

A plant scientist created a new hybrid grass by crossing a desert grass with a shade grass. To determine the new plant's ideal growing conditions, an experiment will be performed in which the hybrid grass is grown in four planters. Each planter will be given the amounts of sunshine and water shown in the diagram below. As part of the procedure, the average height of the hybrid grass in each planter will be recorded every week.

PLANTERS CONTAINING HYBRID GRASS SEEDS

A
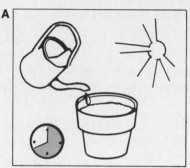
Watered three times each week.

Receives 8 hours or more sunshine each day.

B

Watered three times each week.

Receives 4 hours or less sunshine each day.

C
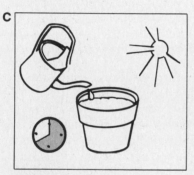
Watered once every two weeks.

Receives 8 hours or more sunshine each day.

D
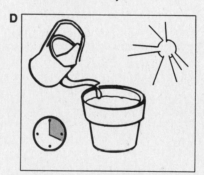
Watered once every two weeks.

Receives 4 hours or less sunshine each day.

6. Which of the following must be assumed to be true if the experiment is to give meaningful results?

   A. The same number of grass seeds must be planted in each planter.

   B. Planters A and B must be given exactly the same amount of water at each watering.

   C. Planters B and C must be given exactly the same amount of sunshine each day.

   (1) A only
   (2) A and B only
   (3) A and C only
   (4) B and C only
   (5) A, B, and C

7. Which of the following conditions, if not met, would *least* affect the results of the experiment?

   (1) The depth of the soil should be identical in all four planters.
   (2) The drainage holes of all four planters should be identical.
   (3) All four planters should be exactly the same diameter (distance across).
   (4) The same type of soil should be placed in all four planters.
   (5) Each planter should be kept free of weeds and destructive insects.

ANSWERS ARE ON PAGE 82.

8. Which two planters should be compared in order to determine the effect of water on the growth of the hybrid grass when it receives full days of sunshine?

    (1) A and B
    (2) A and C
    (3) B and C
    (4) B and D
    (5) C and D

9. Which two planters should be compared in order to determine the effect of sunshine on the growth of the hybrid grass when it is watered only once every two weeks?

    (1) A and B
    (2) A and C
    (3) B and C
    (4) B and D
    (5) C and D

10. Which of the following questions will be *impossible* to answer based on the results of the experiment?

    A. Given the same amount of sunshine, does the amount of water affect the rate at which the hybrid grass grows?

    B. Given the same amount of sunshine, does fertilizer affect the rate at which the hybrid grass grows?

    C. Given the same amount of water, does the amount of sunshine affect the rate at which the hybrid grass grows?

    (1) A only
    (2) B only
    (3) C only
    (4) A and B only
    (5) B and C only

11. The fact that cool water contains more dissolved oxygen than warm water is important in the lives of many water animals. Trout, for example, survive best in water that is shaded and kept cool by overhanging branches. They either die in or leave water that is constantly warmed by sunshine.

    The best explanation for the observation about trout is that warm water

    (1) contains less carbon dioxide than cool water
    (2) carries odors better, which enables predators to more easily find trout
    (3) contains less carbon monoxide than cool water
    (4) tends to flow more quickly than cool water
    (5) contains less oxygen than cool water

12. Scientists give the name *renewable resource* to any useful substance in the environment that can be replaced after it is used up. Food is an example of a renewable resource. Nonrenewable resources are substances that cannot be replaced, like petroleum (oil).

    Which of the following would be classified as a renewable resource?

    (1) coal
    (2) iron
    (3) diamonds
    (4) forests
    (5) natural gas

ANSWERS ARE ON PAGE 82.

Questions 13–15 are based on the following graph.

The graph below represents the amount of light absorbed by chlorophyll. Chlorophyll is the pigment in plant leaves. It traps energy from the sun for use in photosynthesis and gives leaves their green color.

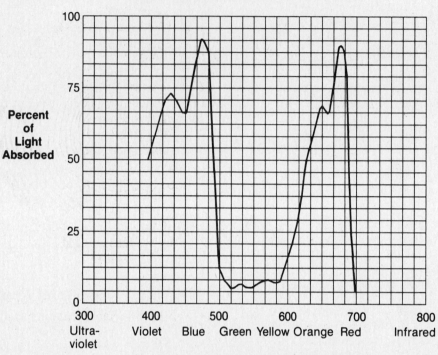

LIGHT ABSORPTION OF CHLOROPHYLL

Wavelength of Light (in nanometers)

13. The two colors of light most absorbed by chlorophyll are

    (1) blue and green
    (2) green and yellow
    (3) blue and reddish orange
    (4) yellow and reddish orange
    (5) violet and infrared

14. Each of the following plants would have a light-absorption graph similar to the graph above *except*

    (1) broccoli
    (2) lettuce
    (3) mushrooms
    (4) lawn grass
    (5) ferns

15. Color is determined by light that is reflected (not absorbed). From the information on the graph, you can conclude that the color of chlorophyll results mainly from light of which of the following wavelengths?

    A. 400 to 500 nanometers
    B. 500 to 600 nanometers
    C. 600 to 700 nanometers

    (1) A only
    (2) B only
    (3) C only
    (4) A and B only
    (5) A and C only

ANSWERS ARE ON PAGE 82.

16. Animals living in the wild have a shorter life expectancy than animals raised in captivity. This is probably because animals in the wild

(1) age more slowly
(2) have scheduled feeding times
(3) are more likely to be killed by predators
(4) have less room in which to exercise
(5) have more stress

17. Each year of its life, a tree grows by adding a new layer of cells to the outside of its stem (trunk). As shown below, these layers form a pattern of growth rings which can be seen by looking at a cross-section of the tree.

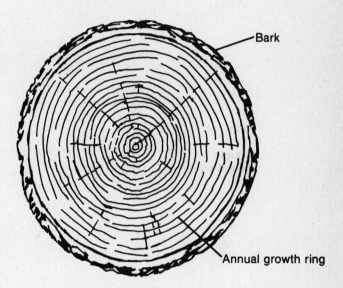

You can conclude that the approximate age of the tree represented above is

(1) 5 years
(2) 13 years
(3) 20 years
(4) 34 years
(5) 47 years

ANSWERS ARE ON PAGE 82.

Questions 18–21 refer to the following information and graph.

A wildlife biologist placed a number of young trout in a lake that previously had no trout in it. The graph below shows the growth of the trout population over many years. It also takes into account the population-limiting factors, things that kill trout before they reach the end of their natural lifespan.

TROUT POPULATION IN A LAKE

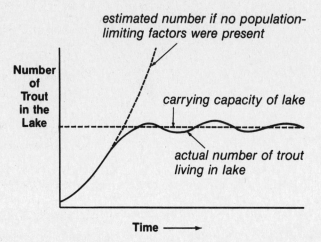

18. According to the graph, population-limiting factors

    (1) tend to be greater during winter months than summer months
    (2) lead to a relatively stable number of trout in the lake
    (3) depend on the size and location of a lake
    (4) increase as the number of trout increases
    (5) affect trout more than they affect smaller fish

19. You can infer from the graph that the *carrying capacity* of the lake is

    (1) the number of trout that the lake can support
    (2) the exact number of trout living in the lake at any one time
    (3) the maximum number of trout that could live in the lake if there were no population-limiting factors
    (4) the average number of trout that die each year
    (5) the average number of trout that are born each year

20. Each of the following is a population-limiting factor *except*

    (1) water pollution in the lake
    (2) bacteria in the lake that can cause fish diseases
    (3) a lack of adequate food resources in the lake for trout
    (4) the presence of larger fish in the lake that feed on trout
    (5) the average lifespan of trout in the lake

21. What would be the most likely result if the Forest Service allowed summer homes to be built along the shores of the lake?

    (1) The carrying capacity of the lake would increase.
    (2) The number of population-limiting factors would decrease.
    (3) The size of the lake would decrease.
    (4) The carrying capacity of the lake would decrease.
    (5) The number of trout living in the lake would increase.

ANSWERS ARE ON PAGE 82.

Questions 22–24 are based on the following information.

Can bacteria live without oxygen? The answer depends on the type of bacteria. Aerobic bacteria can survive only in places where oxygen is plentiful. Anaerobic bacteria, on the other hand, are found only where oxygen is limited or entirely absent. An example is tetanus, which can live in puncture wounds. A third type of bacteria, called *facultative bacteria*, can survive with or without oxygen. *Escherichia coli*, which is present in the human digestive tract, is an example.

22. In which of the following situations would aerobic bacteria survive?

A. in the lungs of a person who has tuberculosis

B. on the leaves of plants growing in a greenhouse

C. on the surface of a piece of cheese

(1) A only
(2) B only
(3) C only
(4) A and C only
(5) A, B, and C

23. What type(s) of bacteria might be found in the digestive tracts of animals?

(1) aerobic only
(2) aerobic and anaerobic only
(3) aerobic and facultative only
(4) anaerobic and facultative only
(5) aerobic, anaerobic, and facultative

24. Suppose that a biologist is making a hypothesis about life forms that existed on Earth three billion years ago. He believes that there could have been bacteria on Earth at that time. He wants to know whether that bacteria would have been aerobic or anaerobic. What feature of the Earth three billion years ago would the biologist be *most* interested in knowing?

(1) the temperature of the Earth's atmosphere
(2) the Earth's age
(3) the content of the Earth's atmosphere
(4) the types of minerals on the Earth's surface
(5) the temperature of the Earth's surface

Question 25 refers to the drawing below.

FERTILE CHICKEN EGG

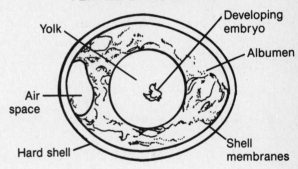

25. Which of the following can you infer from the drawing?

(1) As a chicken embryo gets larger, the yolk gets smaller.
(2) As a chicken embryo gets larger, the albumen gets larger.
(3) Albumen makes up most of the weight of a chicken egg.
(4) The oxygen supply for a developing embryo comes from an air space within its shell.
(5) Except for size, a chicken egg is identical to a duck egg.

ANSWERS ARE ON PAGE 83.

Questions 26–28 refer to the following passage.

Certain features of an environment affect the survival of an organism. These features may be living or nonliving.

Living features can be described as biotic factors, nonliving features as abiotic factors. The availability of food that an animal needs to grow would be a biotic factor, as would be (in a negative way) the presence of predators that feed on an organism. The quality of the air is an abiotic factor that affects the growth of an organism.

26. You can infer from the passage that an organism's best chance for long-term survival depends on

   (1) the presence of all biotic and abiotic factors
   (2) the presence of only certain biotic factors
   (3) the presence of only certain abiotic factors
   (4) the presence of only certain biotic and abiotic factors
   (5) the absence of all biotic and abiotic factors

27. Each of the following is an abiotic factor *except*

   (1) mineral content of soil
   (2) disease-causing bacteria
   (3) air temperature
   (4) water purity
   (5) moisture content of soil

28. In which of the following are both the biotic and abiotic factors controlled in such as way as to best ensure the survival of all animals involved?

   (1) a zoo
   (2) a national park
   (3) a forest
   (4) a museum
   (5) a sheltered bay

ANSWERS ARE ON PAGE 83.

Questions 29 and 30 refer to the following illustration.

RECENT EXTINCTION OF LARGE MAMMALS ONCE NATIVE TO NORTH AMERICA

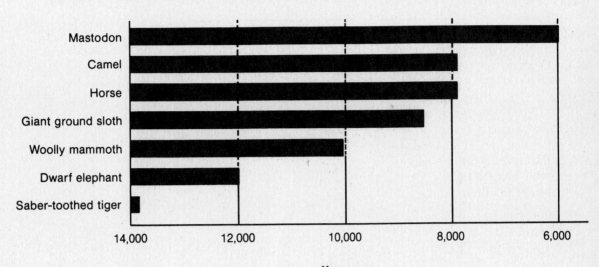

Years ago

29. Which of the following is a restatement of information from the graph above?

(1) For the time shown, the mastodon competed with the woolly mammoth for food.

(2) Of the animals listed, the saber-toothed tiger was the last to become extinct in North America.

(3) The native camel and horse became extinct in North America at about the same time.

(4) The giant ground sloth had a longer life expectancy than the dwarf elephant.

(5) Mammals are more likely to become extinct than reptiles are.

30. Each of the following is a factor that could lead to the extinction of an animal species in North America *except*

(1) the disappearance of food resources

(2) a rise in the number of predators

(3) an extreme temperature change

(4) a rise in air pollution levels

(5) the extinction of similar animals in Europe

ANSWERS ARE ON PAGE 83.

Questions 31 and 32 are based on the information and chart below.

Biologists group all living things into levels of classification. The table below shows the classification scheme of erect mammals.

CLASSIFICATION LEVELS	CLASSIFICATION OF ERECT MAMMALS	CHARACTERISTICS	EXAMPLES
KINGDOM	Animalia	all multicellular animals; specialized tissue and complex organ systems	all microscopic organisms, mammals, reptiles, birds, amphibians, insects, fish, sea squirts, lancelets, worms, jellyfish, and snails
PHYLUM	Chordata	notochord present at some time; replaced by vertebral column in many forms	all mammals, reptiles, birds, amphibians, insects, fish, sea squirts, and lancelets
SUBPHYLUM	Vertebrata	animals with a spinal column (backbone) that encloses a spinal cord	all mammals, reptiles, birds, amphibians, insects, and fish
CLASS	Mammalia	body covered with hair; warm-blooded; lung breathing; mammary glands	mammals only: kangaroos, moles, bats, rabbits, lions, horses, monkeys, and human beings
ORDER	Primates	erect mammals	only certain mammals: monkeys, gorillas, and human beings

31. You can infer from the chart that the level of classification containing the greatest variety of animals is

(1) kingdom
(2) phylum
(3) subphylum
(4) class
(5) order

32. In which of the following levels of classification do both snakes and monkeys belong?

A. Animalia
B. Chordata
C. Vertebrata
D. Mammalia
E. Primates

(1) A only
(2) A and B only
(3) A, B, and C only
(4) A, B, C, and D only
(5) A, B, C, D, and E

ANSWERS ARE ON PAGE 83.

Questions 33–36 refer to the following passage.

Natural mimicry is the resemblance that one organism has to another. Protective mimicry improves the imitator's chances for survival. For example, a harmless, defenseless animal may be protected from predators by its resemblance to an animal that predators tend to avoid.

An example is the viceroy butterfly, which resembles the monarch butterfly. Because the monarch butterfly apparently has an unpleasant taste, birds do not eat it. As a result, birds also avoid the viceroy, even though scientists have discovered in laboratory experiments that birds do in fact enjoy eating viceroys. It seems that, in the wild, birds are unwilling to take the chance of mistaking a monarch for a viceroy.

A second type of mimicry is shown by bola spiders. Bolas are well known for their ability to imitate a female moth's sexual scent. Then, when male moths fly close by, the spider hurls its bola—a ball of glue hanging from its leg—and traps the male moth. The spider wraps the captured moth in silk and devours it.

33. Which of the following best summarizes the passage above?

(1) Butterflies and spiders are similar in the way they use mimicry.
(2) Birds cannot distinguish a viceroy butterfly from a monarch butterfly.
(3) Birds are less intelligent than butterflies, and moths are less intelligent than spiders.
(4) Mimicry is a way in which some organisms gain survival advantages.
(5) Birds and moths do not have very keen senses of vision and smell.

34. Which of the following statements is a hypothesis that would be difficult to prove?

(1) The bola spider uses its bola to trap male moths.
(2) Birds experience the sense of taste in a way similar to the way humans experience taste.
(3) A bola spider gives off a scent that is chemically similar to that given off by female moths.
(4) The visual markings of a viceroy butterfly are similar to those of a monarch butterfly.
(5) There are chemical differences between the body of a monarch and the body of a viceroy.

35. The robber fly looks much like a bumblebee. Considering that robber flies eat bumblebees, apparently the robber fly is

(1) attracted to flowers where it can lay its eggs
(2) accepted by other robber flies and shares in their food supply
(3) accepted by other insects as it looks for bumblebees
(4) mistaken for a bumblebee and is not feared by bumblebees
(5) rejected by birds that might otherwise eat it

36. Which of the following is an inference that can be drawn from the passage?

(1) Birds in captivity will kill and eat monarch butterflies.
(2) Viceroy and monarch butterflies are completely identical to one another.
(3) Bola spiders do not weave webs to trap insects.
(4) Male moths mistake the appearance of a bola spider for a female moth.
(5) A moth in captivity would eat a viceroy butterfly.

ANSWERS ARE ON PAGE 83.

Questions 37–41 refer to the following information.

In order to determine the effectiveness of five types of fertilizer, corn was planted in thirty-five test rows. For each brand of fertilizer, seven rows were planted, each row prepared with a different amount of fertilizer. The results are recorded in the chart below.

Average Corn Plant Height Per Row
(measured in inches)
AMOUNT OF FERTILIZER USED ON EACH ROW

		12 oz.	14 oz.	16 oz.	18 oz.	20 oz.	22 oz.	24 oz.
	A	6	7	9	13	11	10	7
	B	3	4	6	8	9	7	5
FERTILIZER	C	7	8	10	12	14	15	12
BRANDS	D	6	7	8	8	7	6	5
	E	5	7	9	12	13	12	9

37. The tallest crop was achieved with

(1) Brand A fertilizer, using 18 ounces per row
(2) Brand B fertilizer, using 20 ounces per row
(3) Brand C fertilizer, using 22 ounces per row
(4) Brand D fertilizer, using 16 ounces per row
(5) Brand E fertilizer, using 20 ounces per row

38. Listed from greatest growth to least growth, which of the following rates the fertilizers when applied at an amount of 20 ounces per row?

(1) D, E, A, B, C
(2) E, A, C, B, D
(3) C, E, A, B, D
(4) B, C, A, E, D
(5) A, C, E, B, D

39. In order to draw correct conclusions from the experimental results, you must assume each of the following *except* that

(1) each row receives the same amount of sunshine
(2) each row receives the same amount of water
(3) the rows are at least three feet apart
(4) the same type of corn is planted in each row
(5) the corn was planted in each row on the same day

40. Which of the following conclusions is *best* supported by information from the chart?

(1) Too much fertilizer interferes with plant growth.
(2) The more fertilizer used, the taller plants will grow.
(3) All of the fertilizers tested are equally effective.
(4) The amount of water that plants receive is more important to plant growth than the amount of sunshine.
(5) Fertilizer is more important to plant growth than water or sunshine.

41. Which of the following is a statement whose accuracy *cannot* be checked by scientific experiments?

(1) Fertilizer can be used to increase the rate at which plants grow.
(2) Food grown with fertilizer can be chemically different from food grown without fertilizer.
(3) Food that is grown without fertilizer tastes better than food grown with fertilizer.
(4) Fertilizer itself can be harmful to animals that may eat it.
(5) Using too much fertilizer can be more harmful than not using fertilizer at all.

ANSWERS ARE ON PAGE 83.

Human Biology

Text pages
113–143

Questions 1–6 refer to the passage below.

During the spring of 1985, an epidemic of food poisoning in the Midwest focused national attention on a disease known as salmonellosis. More than 18,000 people contracted the disease from improperly pasteurized milk from an Illinois dairy. At least one person died. Since then, there have been a number of smaller but highly publicized outbreaks of the disease involving eggs, cantaloupes, and hamburgers.

Salmonellosis is caused by rod-shaped bacteria called salmonella that are present in moist, protein-rich foods. These foods include raw meat and poultry, milk and milk products, and eggs and egg products. Salmonella bacteria are present in saliva and in fecal matter and are often carried by flies, other insects, and household pets.

Salmonella can usually be destroyed by proper cooking and by maintaining good hygiene. However, salmonella can easily contaminate foods that are not refrigerated.

Food poisoning from salmonella is most common during summer months and is often contracted at cookouts and barbecues where food handling and hygiene may be careless. To reduce chances of salmonella poisoning, one should refrigerate perishable foods and make sure that those who handle the food clean their hands.

1. Which of the following foods is *not* likely to carry the salmonella bacteria?

   (1) oysters   (4) potato salad
   (2) duck eggs   (5) salted crackers
   (3) cottage cheese

2. During which of the following months is the risk of salmonellosis the greatest in the United States?

   (1) May   (4) January
   (2) July   (5) March
   (3) November

3. Suppose that you are packing a picnic cooler with hamburger, bottles of soda pop, ice, and candy bars. Remembering that cold air settles and heat rises, which of the following is the *best* order in which to pack the cooler, starting with the item to be placed on the bottom of the cooler?

   (1) hamburger, soda pop, candy bars, ice
   (2) soda pop, candy bars, ice, hamburger
   (3) soda pop, ice, candy bars, hamburger
   (4) ice, soda pop, candy bars, hamburger
   (5) ice, soda pop, hamburger, candy bars

4. Each of the following is a possible source of salmonella *except*

   (1) an outdoor bathroom with no running water
   (2) a dirty picnic table
   (3) flies buzzing around nearby garbage cans
   (4) a campsite with no central cooking area
   (5) babies in need of frequent diaper changes

5. A family at an afternoon barbecue wants to be protected against food poisoning. The family members need to do each of the following *except*

   (1) clean the picnic table before setting eating utensils down
   (2) thoroughly cook chicken and hamburger before serving
   (3) clean the surface of the grill before cooking
   (4) toast the hamburger buns before making sandwiches
   (5) keep vegetable dips in cooled containers

6. To best prevent the possibility of food poisoning, a shopper should carefully check each food item for the

   (1) sugar content per serving
   (2) types of flavor additives it contains
   (3) date when it was produced
   (4) number of calories per serving
   (5) date after which it should not be sold

ANSWERS ARE ON PAGE 84.

15

Questions 7–10 refer to the passage below.

With the discovery that x-rays pose a radiation risk to patients, medical researchers in recent years looked for a safer non-surgical way for doctors to see inside the human body. Their work led to the invention of ultrasound imaging, a method that does not produce harmful radiation. Ultrasound imaging is the use of sound waves to produce a computer-generated picture of an internal body organ. The technique is based on the same principle as sonar, the use of sound waves by ships to detect underwater objects like sunken vessels or moving submarines.

As a medical tool, ultrasound imaging works especially well for generating pictures of tissue and organs that are primarily composed of fluid. It does not work well for either gases or solid objects such as bones, which conduct sound waves poorly.

So far, ultrasound has proven to be most valuable in diagnosing certain health problems of fetuses and babies. For example, ultrasound can be used to determine the condition of the fetus of a woman in premature labor. Doctors can determine if the fetal lungs are sufficiently developed to enable the fetus to breathe air on its own. With this information, doctors can decide whether to allow the labor to continue or to delay it by using appropriate drugs.

Ultrasound can also be used to diagnose illnesses in babies, and it can be especially useful in monitoring heart problems in infants. Another advantage of ultrasound imaging is the low cost of the equipment and the relative ease with which it is used.

7. Ultrasound imaging was developed in response to concerns over the

(1) cost of x-rays
(2) safety of sonar
(3) safety of x-rays
(4) accuracy of x-ray diagnosis of bone injuries
(5) accuracy of sonar for detecting foreign submarines

8. Computerized tomography (CT)—a form of imaging done by computer analysis of x-ray pictures—is considered to be the best technique available for making images of bones. For which two of the following injuries would you expect CT to give the clearest images of affected parts?

A. a compound fracture of the lower arm
B. torn ligaments in the knee
C. bruised shoulder muscles
D. a broken leg

(1) A and B
(2) A and C
(3) A and D
(4) B and C
(5) B and D

9. For which of the following would sound imaging techniques be *least* likely to be used?

(1) to detect a sunken treasure chest
(2) to warn an airplane of a possible collision
(3) to check the position of a fetus before birth
(4) to locate a submarine
(5) to determine the size of an athlete's heart

10. Which of the following statements is an opinion and not a scientific fact?

(1) Both ultrasound imaging and sonar use sound waves.
(2) Ultrasound imaging will eventually replace x-rays in all imaging needs of a hospital.
(3) Ultrasound imaging does not produce harmful radiation.
(4) The earliest successful uses of ultrasound imaging techniques have been with fetuses and small children.
(5) Ultrasound imaging works well in fluids because sound waves are easily conducted through fluids.

ANSWERS ARE ON PAGE 84.

Questions 11 and 12 refer to the following illustration.

TOP VIEW OF HUMAN SKULL

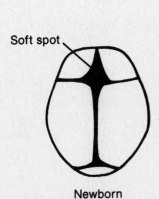 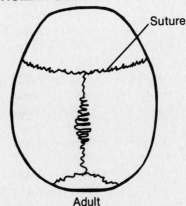

Soft spot

Suture

Newborn

Adult

The membrane between the separate plates of bone in the human skull slowly disappears as an infant grows. In an adult the skull pieces are completely fused together.

11. The soft spot on a baby's head can best be described as

(1) a region of bone that is softer than other regions of bone on the human head

(2) a region on an infant's head where the several bones of the skull have not yet grown together

(3) a hole in the skull of an infant resulting from a bone disease

(4) a temporary birthmark on the skin that covers an infant's skull

(5) a tear in the skin of an infant's skull that occurs during childbirth

12. You can conclude from the diagrams that a person should be careful not to touch a baby's soft spot because

(1) no protective bone lies between the soft spot and the baby's brain

(2) the skin over the soft spot is very sensitive to pain

(3) the soft spot is more apt to get a rash than other skin on the baby's head

(4) a soft spot will get larger if it is touched

(5) a soft spot will not close as quickly if it is often touched

ANSWERS ARE ON PAGE 84.

Questions 13–15 are based on the passage below.

Two million Americans suffer from some form of epilepsy. Epilepsy is a disorder of certain nerve cells in the brain. When functioning normally, these cells produce a small amount of electrical energy that flows through the nervous system and activates body muscles. However, during an epileptic seizure, these cells suddenly release abnormal bursts of electrical energy which the brain cannot control.

In the more severe type of epilepsy, victims may lose consciousness and fall down, shaking uncontrollably. This type of seizure often lasts several minutes. In a much milder form, victims lose awareness of their surroundings for a few seconds but do not fall or lose consciousness.

Scientists do not understand what causes epilepsy, but they do know that it cannot be spread from one person to another. Moreover, doctors are now able to treat epilepsy with drugs that either reduce the frequency of seizures or prevent them entirely. Most people who have epilepsy can now lead normal lives.

13. An epileptic seizure is best described as

   (1) a temporary loss of conscious awareness or of body control due to an electrical disturbance in the brain
   (2) a permanent loss of conscious awareness or of body control due to an electrical disturbance in the brain
   (3) an electrical disturbance in the brain caused by a loss of body control
   (4) a permanent mental condition caused by severe bodily injury
   (5) an injury to the body caused by a fall that occurs because of a brain malfunction

14. Each phrase below describes epilepsy *except*

   (1) an electrical malfunction in the brain
   (2) a condition characterized by loss of body control
   (3) a contagious disease
   (4) a condition accompanied by a temporary seizure
   (5) a condition that's usually controllable with medicine

15. With medical treatment, most epileptics can lead normal working lives. However, those who have severe seizures that are only partially controllable may be limited in employment opportunities.

   Which of the following jobs would be a poor choice for a person who has occasional seizures that can be only partly controlled by medicine?

   (1) computer programmer
   (2) salesperson
   (3) writer
   (4) bus driver
   (5) janitor

ANSWERS ARE ON PAGE 84.

Questions 16 and 17 refer to the following diagram.

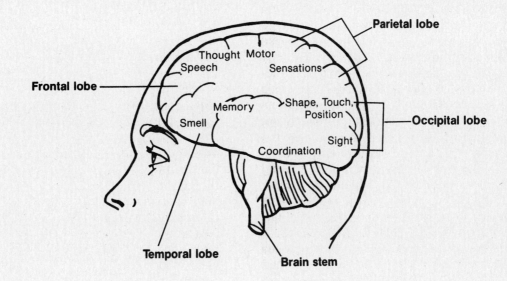

16. The part of the brain that is involved in vision is the

   (1) frontal lobe
   (2) parietal lobe
   (3) temporal lobe
   (4) occipital lobe
   (5) brain stem

17. Which statement *best* summarizes the information in the illustration?

   (1) All human brains are nearly identical in size.
   (2) Specific parts of the brain control specific body functions.
   (3) Intelligence is determined by brain size.
   (4) The surface of the brain contains many folds.
   (5) The brain stem connects the spinal cord to the brain.

18. Although unpleasant, pain and discomfort can serve a purpose: they can warn us that some of our activities are stressful or unhealthy. For instance, back pain is often a signal that we have been sitting or standing in a position that is bad for the back. If we do not pay attention to this warning and change our posture, the pain may get much worse.

Which of the following types of pain or discomfort is *not* merely a warning caused by a particular activity or type of behavior?

   (1) stiffness from sleeping in an awkward position
   (2) sore muscles from exercising much more than usual
   (3) stomachache after eating too much at a meal
   (4) discomfort while recovering from major surgery
   (5) pain felt when accidentally touching a hot stove burner

ANSWERS ARE ON PAGE 84.

Questions 19–23 are based on the passage below.

   Despite the popularity of brushing and flossing and the countless dollars we spend on mouthwash, billions of bacteria call our mouths home—and our tongues are the welcome mat.

   According to Alan Drinnan, professor of oral medicine at the University of Buffalo School of Dentistry, we should add daily tongue cleaning to our oral hygiene routine. "People are always surprised at the amount of debris they remove this way," he says. The procedure cuts down on bacteria and leftover food particles, both implicated in tooth decay, periodontal disease, and bad breath.

   It is only in the past century that we have neglected our tongues. Throughout the 1700s and 1800s, Europeans used tongue scrapers, often elaborate silver ones. And archeologists have unearthed Roman tongue scrapers dating to A.D. 100.

   While there are at least six different scrapers now on the market, Drinnan says it's just as easy to use the edge of a spoon, gently pulling it across the tongue.

—From *Science Digest*

19. Which statement *best* summarizes the passage above?

   (1) Tongue scraping has been around for centuries.
   (2) An inexpensive tongue scraper is as close as your spoon.
   (3) People are surprised that tongue scraping removes bacteria.
   (4) Tongue scraping is better for teeth than brushing or flossing.
   (5) Tongue scraping improves overall oral hygiene.

20. Which of the following can be inferred from information given in the article?

   (1) Ancient Romans had little or no tooth decay.
   (2) Since at least the eighteenth century, people have known that tongue scraping removes harmful bacteria from the mouth.
   (3) Tongue scraping has no serious side effects for the taste buds located on the tongue.

   (4) Tongue scraping is more effective at preventing tooth decay than is brushing or flossing.
   (5) Modern dentistry owes its beginning to discoveries made in the 1700s and 1800s.

21. Scraping does for the tongue what

   (1) good nutrition does for the body
   (2) exercise does for the body
   (3) a massage does for the body
   (4) bathing does for the body
   (5) sunshine does for the body

22. Which of the following statements is most likely a hypothesis that is *not* directly supported by evidence?

   (1) Leftover food particles can get trapped in tiny folds in the tongue's surface.
   (2) Ancient Romans scraped their tongues in hopes of preventing tooth decay and gum disease.
   (3) A spoon can be effectively used as a tongue scraper.
   (4) Bacterial growth is aided by leftover food particles that remain on the tongue.
   (5) Brushing and flossing alone do not remove all harmful bacteria from a person's mouth.

23. Which of the following studies would provide the best evidence that tongue scraping can reduce tooth decay in young children?
   A study of two groups of young children: one group that brushes, flosses, and scrapes their tongues, and a second group that

   (1) brushes and flosses only
   (2) brushes, flosses, and scrapes their tongues
   (3) does not brush, floss, or scrape their tongues
   (4) scrapes their tongues only
   (5) flosses only

ANSWERS ARE ON PAGE 84.

Questions 24 and 25 are based on the following chart.

Recommended Daily Vitamin Needs of Adults

(based on American Medical Association figures)

Vitamin A	5000 IU
Vitamin D	400 IU
Vitamin E	30 IU
Vitamin C	60 mg
Folic Acid	0.4 mg
Thiamine	1.5mg
Riboflavin	1.7mg
Niacin	20 mg
Vitamin B₆	2 mg
Vitamin B₁₂	6 mcg

mg = milligram
IU = international units
mcg = microgram

24. Which of the following can be inferred from information given on the chart above?

(1) Vitamin A is more necessary than the other vitamins listed.
(2) International units (IU) are larger than milligrams (mg).
(3) For good health, the human body needs a variety of vitamins.
(4) Children have the same vitamin needs as adults.
(5) Vitamin A is important for night vision.

25. Which of the following statements is an opinion?

(1) Unlike human beings, many animals can produce their own supply of vitamin C.
(2) Vitamin deficiency can lead to many types of illnesses.
(3) Snacks such as fruit and nuts contain more essential vitamins than candy.
(4) All children should take vitamin supplements in order to develop properly.
(5) Both minerals and vitamins are essential for good health.

26. Which of the following facts is *least* relevant to the relationship between the consumption of alcohol and health?

(1) Alcohol affects some body organs more than others.
(2) People who drink a lot tend to ignore their nutritional needs.
(3) When pregnant women drink alcohol, the developing fetus can be harmed.
(4) Seventy percent of drivers killed in one-car accidents had been drinking alcohol shortly before the accident.
(5) One can of beer contains the same amount of alcohol as one glass of wine.

Question 27 is based on the illustration below.

THE HUMAN TOOTH

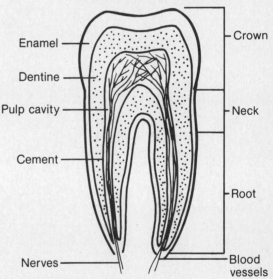

27. The protective outer layer of the tooth is known as the

(1) crown
(2) neck
(3) root
(4) enamel
(5) dentine

ANSWERS ARE ON PAGE 85.

Questions 28–30 are based on the following information and graph.

The three major structural tissues in a human body are fat, muscle, and bone. Fat can be either of two types: essential fat or storage fat. Essential fat is stored in bone marrow and in organs. Storage fat is the type we usually think of as excess fat, since it often adds unwanted weight to our bodies. Storage fat is made up of fatty tissue that surrounds internal organs or is deposited beneath the skin.

The circle graphs below compare the body composition of an average-sized young man with that of an average-sized young woman.

BODY COMPOSITION
(percent of total weight)

AVERAGE-SIZED YOUNG MAN

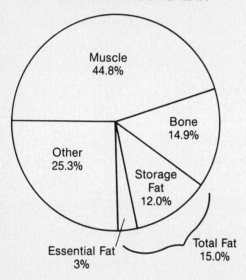

AVERAGE-SIZED YOUNG WOMAN

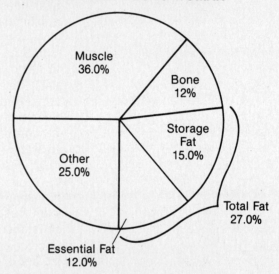

28. You can see from the graphs that, compared to an average-sized young woman, an average-sized young man has a higher percent of

   (1) total fat and bone
   (2) bone and muscle
   (3) total fat and muscle
   (4) bone only
   (5) muscle only

29. Which of the following statements is best supported by information in the passage and on the graphs above?

   (1) Overweight women eat more sweets than overweight men.
   (2) Overweight women get less exercise than overweight men.
   (3) Slim women have the same percent of total fat as slim men.
   (4) Slim women have a higher percent of total fat than slim men.
   (5) Overweight women have a harder time losing weight than overweight men.

30. As shown on the graph, women have a higher percentage of total fat than men. The most reasonable explanation for this fact is that women

   (1) do less physical labor than men
   (2) need more fat to protect larger reproductive organs
   (3) have broader hips
   (4) have larger appetites
   (5) feel pressured by society to go on diets

ANSWERS ARE ON PAGE 85.

Questions 31–34 refer to the passage below.

Under normal conditions, human beings maintain a relatively constant body temperature—about 98.6° F. Humans can become very ill or even die when body temperature changes too much from its normal level.

Heatstroke (sunstroke) occurs when the temperature-regulating system of the body ceases to work effectively. When people work in extreme heat, they may stop sweating—the body's natural way of cooling itself. The skin becomes hot and dry, and body temperature rises above normal. Other symptoms may include irregular heartbeat and shallow, irregular breathing. The victim usually becomes unconscious.

Because the high body temperatures of heatstroke can cause brain damage and death, heatstroke should be treated immediately. Standard treatment is to quickly reduce body temperature by applying cold compresses to the victim's body and ice packs to the neck. If possible, the victim should be placed in a bathtub full of cold water. Only when body temperature is down to 102° F should the cooling procedures be stopped.

Heat exhaustion is less serious than heatstroke. With heat exhaustion, a victim becomes weak and dizzy after working in high temperature and high humidity. Other symptoms include confusion, an abnormal secretion of sweat, and a body temperature *below* normal. Proper treatment includes moving the victim to a cooler location but keeping the victim warm until body temperature rises to normal.

To help avoid both heatstroke and heat exhaustion, people who work in hot and possibly humid conditions should drink plenty of water and take frequent rest breaks in order to cool off.

31. From information given in the passage, you can infer that proper treatment for heat exhaustion may include

   (1) covering the victim with a blanket
   (2) placing an ice pack on the victim's chest
   (3) checking the blood sugar level of the victim
   (4) giving the victim a drink of ice water
   (5) placing the victim in a sitting position

32. As a protective health measure, the most important thing for an exercise club to maintain in good working order is its

   (1) toilets
   (2) door locks
   (3) window locks
   (4) clocks
   (5) drinking fountains

33. From information given in the passage, you can reasonably conclude that the purpose of applying ice packs to the neck of a heatstroke victim is to

   (1) slow the flow of blood to the brain
   (2) reduce excess heat energy by inducing shivering
   (3) cool the neck and shoulder muscles
   (4) cool the blood flowing to the brain
   (5) prevent convulsions by cooling the nervous system

34. A doctor comes to the assistance of a middle-aged woman who collapsed while working outdoors on a hot afternoon. Each of the following will be a clue to what is wrong with the woman *except* the

   (1) woman's exact age
   (2) woman's body temperature
   (3) woman's blood pressure
   (4) woman's heart rate
   (5) regularity of the woman's breathing

ANSWERS ARE ON PAGE 85.

Questions 35–38 are based on the following graphs.

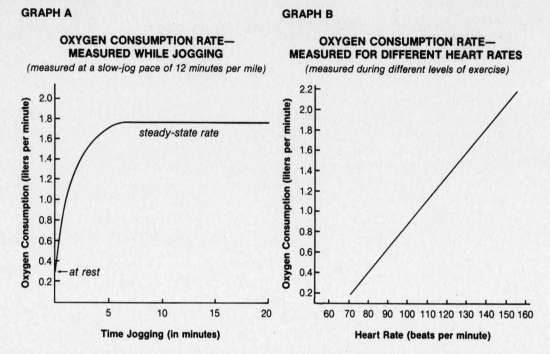

GRAPH A

**OXYGEN CONSUMPTION RATE—
MEASURED WHILE JOGGING**
(measured at a slow-jog pace of 12 minutes per mile)

steady-state rate

←at rest

Oxygen Consumption (liters per minute)

Time Jogging (in minutes)

GRAPH B

**OXYGEN CONSUMPTION RATE—
MEASURED FOR DIFFERENT HEART RATES**
(measured during different levels of exercise)

Oxygen Consumption (liters per minute)

Heart Rate (beats per minute)

The above graphs represent average oxygen-consumption rates of healthy but nonathletic adults.

35. Although heart rates vary from person to person, the average heart rate of a person at rest is about 78 beats per minute. According to either graph A or B, the amount of oxygen consumed per minute by a healthy but nonathletic person at rest is approximately

(1) 0.1 liter
(2) 0.3 liter
(3) 0.8 liter
(4) 1.0 liter
(5) 1.5 liter

36. Which of the following is the best summary of information on graph A?

(1) The steady-state rate of oxygen consumption during jogging depends on the jogger's average speed.
(2) The most rapid increase in oxygen consumption takes place during the first six minutes of jogging.
(3) Oxygen consumption is lower while at rest than during jogging.
(4) Oxygen consumption rises during the first six minutes of jogging to a constant steady-state rate thereafter.
(5) While jogging, different individuals have different steady-state oxygen-consumption rates.

37. Taking information from both graphs, you can conclude that after 10 minutes of slow jogging, a person's heart rate will be

(1) about 100 beats per minute
(2) about 120 beats per minute
(3) about 140 beats per minute
(4) about 160 beats per minute
(5) greater than 160 beats per minute

38. If, after 20 minutes of jogging at a rate of 12 minutes per mile, a person suddenly increases the pace to 11 minutes per mile, what will be the most likely effect on oxygen consumption?

(1) a quick increase to a higher steady-state level
(2) a quick decrease to a lower steady-state level
(3) continuation at the same steady-state level
(4) a steadily rising rate and no new steady-state level
(5) a steadily falling rate and no new steady-state level

ANSWERS ARE ON PAGE 85.

Question 39 refers to the following diagram.

ACTION OF VALVES IN VEINS

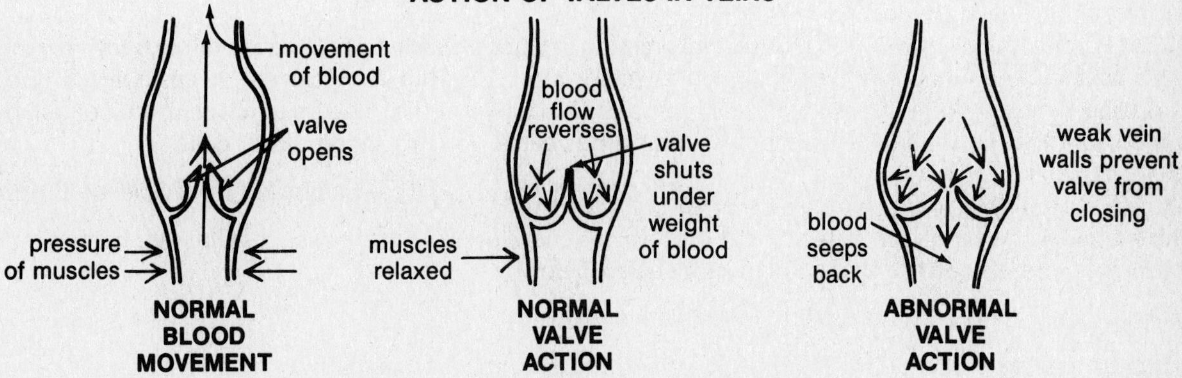

39. As shown in the illustration above, the purpose of valves in veins is to

(1) increase blood pressure
(2) increase the speed of blood flow
(3) restrict the flow of blood to a single direction
(4) enable blood to flow back and forth
(5) transfer blood from arteries to veins

---

40. Lung tissue is damaged when exposed to smoke over a prolonged time. When lung tissue is damaged, less oxygen enters the bloodstream from the lungs during each breath.

Suppose that a smoker and a nonsmoker begin an exercise program together. When compared with the nonsmoker, which of the following would the smoker most likely experience during mild exercise?

(1) a slower breathing rate
(2) less need to rest frequently
(3) muscles tiring more slowly
(4) a smaller amount of perspiration
(5) a more rapidly beating heart

ANSWERS ARE ON PAGE 85.

Questions 41–45 refer to the following information.

Leeches, once considered useful for improving patients' circulation by sucking their blood, seem to be finding a place in modern medicine.

At Pennsylvania Hospital in Philadelphia, oncologist Gabriel Gasic has found that an extract from the saliva of the South American leech, when injected into mice with lung cancer, keeps tumors from spreading. The key, writes Gasic in a recent issue of *Cancer Research*, may be a powerful anticoagulant in the saliva that prevents blood clots—thought to be "nests" for circulating tumor cells.

—Excerpted from *Science Digest*

The statements that follow refer to the discoveries mentioned in the passage. Classify each statement into one of the five categories defined below.

an experiment—a procedure used to investigate a problem

a finding—an experimental result obtained or a conclusion reached as part of the investigation

a hypothesis—a reasonable, but not proven, explanation of an observed fact

a prediction—an opinion about something that may occur in the future

irrelevant information—information that does not directly help the researcher understand the problem being investigated

41. Leeches are aquatic worms that live as parasites, attaching themselves to the skin of fish and other water animals.

This statement is best classified as a(n)

(1) experiment
(2) finding
(3) hypothesis
(4) prediction
(5) irrelevant information

42. Blood clots may serve as nests for circulating cancer cells.

This statement is best classified as a(n)

(1) experiment
(2) finding
(3) hypothesis
(4) prediction
(5) irrelevant information

43. South American leech saliva, when injected into mice with lung cancer, keeps cancer tumors from spreading.

This statement is best classified as a(n)

(1) experiment
(2) finding
(3) hypothesis
(4) prediction
(5) irrelevant information

44. To see how mice respond to leech saliva, Gasic injected the saliva of the South American leech into mice with lung cancer.

This statement describes a(n)

(1) experiment
(2) finding
(3) hypothesis
(4) prediction
(5) irrelevant information

45. Because of its effect as an anticoagulant, leech saliva may someday be used as a medicine to help prevent heart attacks.

This statement is best classified as a(n)

(1) experiment
(2) finding
(3) hypothesis
(4) prediction
(5) irrelevant information

ANSWERS ARE ON PAGE 85.

Questions 46 and 47 refer to the following illustration.

COMPARISON OF HUMAN AND BABOON JAWS

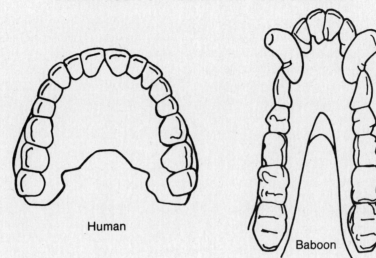

Human

Baboon

46. A human being's jaw is similar to that of a baboon in the

   (1) length of the jaw
   (2) width of the jaw
   (3) number of teeth in the jaw
   (4) shape of teeth in the jaw
   (5) shape of the jawbone

47. Differences between the jaw of a human being and the jaw of a baboon most likely are related to differences in

   (1) intelligence
   (2) lifespan
   (3) breathing
   (4) diet
   (5) communication

ANSWERS ARE ON PAGE 85.

Questions 48–51 refer to the passage below.

Temporary sunburn is the least serious of many health problems risked by sunbathers. In addition to premature wrinkles and forms of skin cancer, overexposure to sunlight may cause several types of eye damage.

Sunlight is actually composed of many different colors of light, each with a particular energy level. Most harmful to the eyes is high-energy light—visible blue and violet light, and invisible ultraviolet light.

The cornea, the transparent outer surface of the eye, helps protect the inner parts of the eye by absorbing much of the sun's ultraviolet light. However, overexposure to bright sunlight can cause *keratitis*, an itchy condition that usually lasts only a day or two. "Snow blindness" and "welder's flash" are two types of keratitis.

Behind the cornea is the lens. The purpose of the lens is to focus light onto the retina at the back of the eye. In some cases, though, ultraviolet light can cause cataracts to form in the lens. Cataracts are cloudy areas that disrupt vision by scattering all visible light.

The retina, the inner layer of the eye, is made up of layers of cells that change light rays to electrical signals that are then sent along the optic nerve to the brain. In recent years, researchers have discovered that prolonged exposure to visible blue and violet light can scar the retina. The risk of this type of injury is greatest to those who work or play continuously in bright sunshine.

48. The key point made by the author in this passage is that

(1) overexposure to sunlight is the main cause of keratitis
(2) sunlight is composed of light of various colors and energies
(3) welders are more sensitive to sunlight than other people are
(4) the eye is made up of several interrelated structures
(5) overexposure to sunlight can result in several types of eye damage

49. According to the passage, an important function of the cornea is to

(1) give the eye color
(2) produce tears to cleanse the eye
(3) protect the lens from dirt
(4) absorb high-energy light rays
(5) send electrical signals to the brain

50. Which of the following activities is *least* likely to put people at risk of retinal damage from overexposure to blue light?

(1) mountain climbing
(2) water skiing
(3) bird watching
(4) driving westward in the late afternoon
(5) reading under a bright lamp

51. The most important health feature of the lenses of sunglasses is their

(1) thickness
(2) filtering property
(3) shape
(4) color
(5) cost

ANSWERS ARE ON PAGE 86.

Questions 52–54 are based on the chart below.

The figures below show the effectiveness of various birth control methods when instructions are followed to the letter. All methods are less effective when not used properly.

BIRTH CONTROL METHOD	EFFECTIVENESS (Approximate percent of women who become pregnant each year while using this method)
Condom	3%
Contraceptive foam	18%
Diaphragm	3½%
Intrauterine device (IUD)	2½%
Birth control pill	1%
Sterilization (tubal ligation or vasectomy)	almost 0%

52. Of the following birth control methods listed in the chart, which is the most effective?

(1) condoms
(2) contraceptive foam
(3) diaphragm
(4) IUD
(5) birth control pill

53. Which of the following is an opinion?

(1) The diaphragm is a more effective birth control device than contraceptive foam.
(2) There are several types of birth control devices on the market.
(3) Teenagers who use birth control are acting sensibly and responsibly.
(4) The price of birth control devices is relatively low.
(5) Health clinics in many communities provide free information on birth control.

54. In which of the following publications would you be *least* likely to find this table?

(1) an advertisement for contraceptive foam
(2) a leaflet put out by a community health center
(3) a book on different forms of birth control
(4) a book on women's health
(5) an advertisement for birth control pills

ANSWERS ARE ON PAGE 86.

Earth Science

Questions 1–5 are based on the following information.

Many common minerals can be identified by one or more of the following five properties.

color—A mineral's color depends on the color of the element(s) that compose it or on the color of impurities it contains.

luster—Luster refers to the degree to which a mineral reflects light. It may be classified as metallic or nonmetallic. A mineral with metallic luster shines like a metal.

hardness—The hardness of a mineral refers to how easily a mineral can be scratched.

streak—Streak refers to the color of the powder that a mineral leaves when it is rubbed against a hard surface.

cleavage—Cleavage refers to the way a mineral breaks or splits and depends on the pattern of the mineral's crystals.

1. Gold prospectors were often fooled by pyrite (fool's gold), a mineral that is bright and shiny like gold. However, there is an easy way to identify pyrite: when pyrite is rubbed against a rock, it leaves a black mark. This distinguishing property of pyrite is classified as

   (1) color   **(4)** streak
   (2) luster   **(5)** cleavage
   (3) hardness

2. To cut blocks of granite, engineers have designed special saw blades that have diamond dust embedded in their steel teeth. Diamonds are useful for cutting because of their

   (1) color   **(4)** streak
   (2) luster   **(5)** cleavage
   (3) hardness

3. Corundum, a mineral that is naturally clear, becomes a red ruby when a small amount of chromium is present. On the other hand, traces of iron and titanium turn a clear crystal of corundum into a blue sapphire. Which property of corundum is *most* affected by traces of other substances?

   (1) color   **(4)** streak
   (2) luster   **(5)** cleavage
   (3) hardness

4. Because of its crystalline structure, a diamond can be split in four separate directions. This allows a diamond to be cut in the shape of a pyramid that brilliantly reflects light in several directions at once. The shape and reflective properties of a cut diamond are determined by its

   (1) color   **(4)** streak
   (2) luster   **(5)** cleavage
   (3) hardness

5. When shined, silver and copper are highly reflective. This property is best classified as

   (1) color   **(4)** streak
   (2) luster   **(5)** cleavage
   (3) hardness

ANSWERS ARE ON PAGE 86.

Questions 6 and 7 refer to the chart below.

Mohs' Scale of Mineral Hardness		
MINERAL	HARDNESS	PROPERTY
Talc	1	can be scratched by a fingernail
Gypsum	2	
Calcite	3	can be scratched by a copper penny
Fluorite	4	can be scratched by a piece of glass
Apatite	5	
Feldspar	6	can scratch a piece of glass or a knife blade
Quartz	7	
Topaz	8	
Corundum	9	
Diamond	10	can scratch all other common materials

6. According to Mohs' scale above, each of the following minerals could be used in a rubbing compound designed to smooth the edges of a roughly cut piece of glass *except*

(1) fluorite
(2) quartz
(3) diamond
(4) feldspar
(5) topaz

7. From information given on Mohs' scale, you can conclude that the hardness rating of a piece of glass is between

(1) 2 and 3
(2) 3 and 4
(3) 4 and 5
(4) 5 and 6
(5) 6 and 7

8. Which of the following is *not* evidence that the Earth is round?

(1) A ship seems to sink out of sight as it sails out on the sea directly away from shore.
(2) The height of a particular star over the horizon is different when viewed from a northern state than when viewed from a southern state.
(3) The shadow of the Earth formed on the moon during a lunar eclipse is a curved line.
(4) Both the sun and full moon appear as round objects in the sky.
(5) People in China can watch the sun come up at the same time that people in the United States watch the sun go down.

ANSWERS ARE ON PAGE 86.

Questions 9–11 are based on the following passage.

Did you ever wonder why cloudy nights are warmer than clear, starlit nights? The answer has to do with how the surface of the Earth is heated and cooled.

During the day, the Earth's surface absorbs much of the sunlight that strikes it. The absorbed light heats land and water masses in much the same way that sunlight warms you. The hotter the day, the more sunlight energy is absorbed, and the hotter the surface becomes.

When the sun goes below the horizon, the air quickly cools. Land and water, however, cool more slowly because they hold much more heat energy. After the sun goes down, this heat energy slowly radiates upward, away from the Earth's surface. On a clear night, most of this energy radiates back into space and is lost.

On a cloudy night, however, clouds absorb heat energy that radiates upward from the Earth's surface. The result is that a layer of clouds acts like a blanket and traps heat energy between the clouds and the Earth's surface, warming the air in between.

9. The key point made in the passage above is that

(1) clouds trap heat that radiates from the Earth's surface
(2) the Earth is warmed by sunshine that strikes its surface
(3) in the evening, air cools more quickly than land or water
(4) clouds form only on warm evenings
(5) clouds trap heat that radiates from the sun to the Earth

10. In which of the following places, all having the same average daytime temperature, would you expect the average nighttime temperature to be the lowest?

(1) along the ocean shore
(2) in a river valley
(3) next to one of the Great Lakes
(4) in a desert
(5) on a small island

11. For which of the following conditions would the nighttime temperatures most likely be the highest?

(1) a totally cloudy day, a totally cloudy night
(2) a partly cloudy day, a totally cloudy night
(3) a clear day, a totally cloudy night
(4) a clear day, a partly cloudy night
(5) a partly cloudy day, a totally clear night

ANSWERS ARE ON PAGE 86.

Question 12 is based on the following graph.

MAIN DISSOLVED SUBSTANCES IN SEA WATER
(by weight)

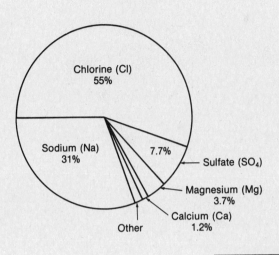

12. From information given on the graph, you can deduce that the main substance dissolved in sea water is

(1) calcium chloride (CaC1$_2$)
(2) magnesium oxide (MgO)
(3) sodium chloride (NaCl)
(4) sulfuric acid (H$_2$SO$_4$)
(5) potassium chloride (KCl)

Questions 13 and 14 are based on the graph below.

The graph shows four temperature readings taken on Sierra Peak, a 10,540-foot-high mountain.

NOVEMBER 9 TEMPERATURE READINGS ON SIERRA PEAK

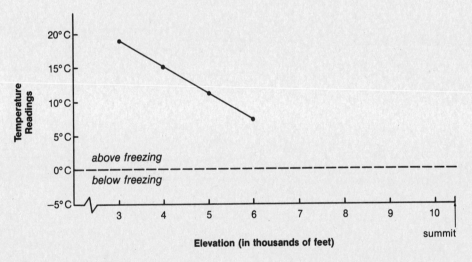

13. Assuming the same rate of temperature decrease at higher elevations, you can infer that the freezing level (0° C) occurs at an elevation that is

(1) below 6,000 feet
(2) about 6,000 feet
(3) about 8,000 feet
(4) about 10,000 feet
(5) above 10,000 feet

14. The person whose plans are *most likely* affected by the information presented on this graph is

(1) a commercial pilot
(2) a fisherman
(3) a map maker
(4) a mountain climber
(5) a construction worker

ANSWERS ARE ON PAGE 86.

Questions 15 and 16 refer to the illustrations below.

NORMAL DAYTIME CONDITIONS

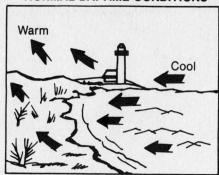

NORMAL NIGHTTIME CONDITIONS

15. You can infer from the illustrations above that the air along a beach is still only when

 (1) the air above the land is cool
 (2) the air above the water is warm
 (3) the air above the land is the same temperature as the air above the water
 (4) the sun is rising or setting
 (5) it is raining over both the land and water

16. Which of the following could cause a reversal in the direction of the daytime breeze?

 (1) unusually cold ocean water
 (2) unusually heavy air pollution over land and water
 (3) thick, early-morning fog over the ocean
 (4) an unusually warm day along the land near the shore
 (5) an unusually cold day along the land near the shore

ANSWERS ARE ON PAGE 86.

Questions 17–19 refer to the information below.

THE ATLANTIC MID-OCEAN RIDGE

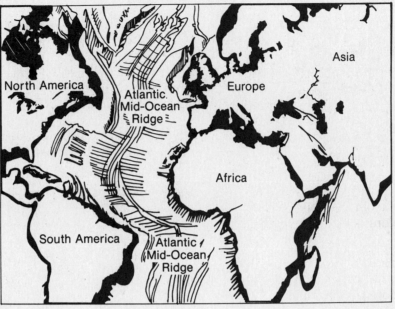

As shown in the drawing above, the Atlantic Mid-Ocean Ridge is a long underwater mountain range that sits about halfway between the continents on either side of it. Scientists believe that the sea floor is spreading outward along this ridge. This spreading seems to be caused by continual eruptions of underwater volcanoes that make up this long mountain chain. The result of the spreading is that the continents of North and South America are moving farther apart from the continents of Europe and Africa.

17. What is the probable cause of the spreading of the sea floor?

(1) The continents are moving farther from the ridge.
(2) The ridge is located approximately midway between the continents to the left and those to the right.
(3) The sea floor is not smooth, but is characterized by high mountain ranges and deep canyons.
(4) New sea floor is being created from liquid rock that is pushed up from the Earth's interior.
(5) North and South America are slowly moving farther from Europe and Africa.

18. Assume that North and South America were once very close to Europe and Africa. What is the best evidence that the spreading of the sea floor occurs at about the same rate on both sides of the ridge?

(1) The shape of South America is similar to the shape of Africa.
(2) The coastline to the left is about the same distance away from the ridge as is the coastline to the right.
(3) The coastline to the left of the ridge has the same general shape as the coastline to the right.
(4) The sea floor to the left of the ridge contains the same types of minerals found on the right.
(5) The ridge is the same general shape as the coastlines of the continents on either side of it.

19. In which of the following studies would information about the Atlantic Mid-Ocean Ridge be of *least* interest?

(1) the effect of ocean temperature on land climate
(2) the migration patterns of ocean animals
(3) undersea mining
(4) ocean current movement
(5) undersea volcanoes

ANSWERS ARE ON PAGE 87.

Questions 20 and 21 refer to the information and drawing below.

As shown in the drawing below, Polaris (called the North Star) is almost directly in line with the Earth's rotation axis.

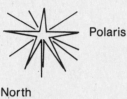

20. At which of the following locations would the North Star appear to be directly over a person standing on Earth?

    (1) the North Pole
    (2) halfway between the equator and the North Pole
    (3) the equator
    (4) halfway between the equator and the South Pole
    (5) the South Pole

21. Anyone who uses the North Star as a direction-finder must assume that the North Star

    (1) is the brightest evening star
    (2) can be located by first locating the group of stars known as the Big Dipper
    (3) is as easily seen during daytime as during nighttime
    (4) stays in the same position in the sky at all hours of the night
    (5) is in the Milky Way Galaxy along with the sun

22. The constellations (patterns of stars) seen in the summer sky are not the same as the constellations seen in the winter sky. Which of the following statements *best* explains this observation?

    (1) There are more hours of nighttime darkness in winter than in summer.
    (2) Constellations have been studied since ancient times.
    (3) The dark side of the Earth points to a different part of space in winter than in summer.
    (4) The noonday sun is higher in the sky in summer than in winter.
    (5) The distance of the Earth from the sun is not the same in winter as it is in summer.

23. A "shooting star"—seen as a brief streak of light across the night sky—is not really a star at all. It is a meteor, a piece of fast-moving matter from space that burns up upon entering the Earth's upper atmosphere.

    Which of the following statements about shooting stars is a scientific hypothesis rather than a fact or an opinion?

    (1) Large numbers of meteors can be seen when the Earth passes a point in space where a comet has passed.
    (2) Shooting stars bring luck to those who see them.
    (3) In some cultures, shooting stars are a religious symbol.
    (4) Pieces of matter in space are most likely tiny fragments of icy materials left behind by passing comets.
    (5) A few shooting stars pass entirely through the atmosphere and strike the Earth.

ANSWERS ARE ON PAGE 87.

Questions 24–26 are based on the following graph.

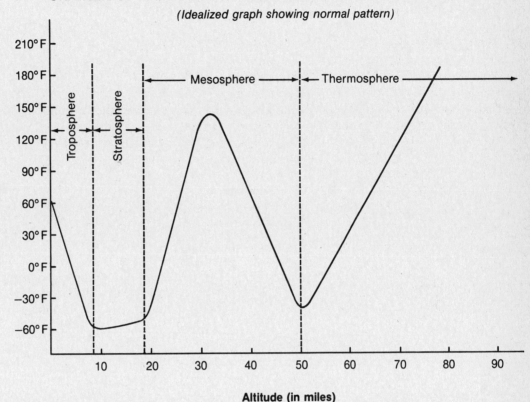

CHANGES OF ATMOSPHERIC TEMPERATURE WITH INCREASING ALTITUDE

(Idealized graph showing normal pattern)

Altitude (in miles)

24. The lowest temperature in the atmosphere occurs at the dividing point between the

   (1) mesosphere and thermosphere
   (2) troposphere and mesosphere
   (3) troposphere and stratosphere
   (4) stratosphere and mesosphere
   (5) stratosphere and thermosphere

25. In which layer of atmosphere does the air temperature at first rise with increasing altitude and, at higher altitudes, decrease as the altitude increases?

   (1) troposphere
   (2) stratosphere
   (3) mesosphere
   (4) thermosphere
   (5) troposphere and thermosphere

26. A commercial airliner, traveling cross country, cruises at an altitude of 33,000 feet (about six miles). Between the time the airliner takes off and the time it reaches its cruising altitude, the air temperature outside of the plane

   (1) continually increases
   (2) continually decreases
   (3) at first decreases and then increases
   (4) at first increases and then decreases
   (5) remains approximately constant

ANSWERS ARE ON PAGE 87.

Questions 27–31 refer to the passage below.

Soil drainage depends on the relative amounts of clay, silt, and sand contained in the soil. Clay particles are typically a few thousandths of a millimeter wide; silt particles are a few hundredths of a millimeter wide; and sand particles are a few tenths of a millimeter wide.

A soil scientist is planning an experiment to test the drainage of different soils obtained from a riverbed. As shown in the illustration below, he has placed samples in each of six containers. He'll now measure the drainage property of each sample by pouring an equal amount of water in each container. He'll then measure the rate at which water flows out the screened bottom of each container.

A — Clay only

B — Silt only

C — Sand only

D — Mixed clay and silt

E — Mixed silt and sand

F — Mixed clay, silt, and sand

27. Which of the following conditions must be met if the experiments are to give meaningful results?

A. Each container contains an equal weight of soil.

B. Before water is added, the soil in each container is dry.

C. The depth of the soil is the same in each container.

(1) A only
(2) B only
(3) A and C only
(4) B and C only
(5) A, B, and C

28. To compare the drainage property of silt with that of sand, the scientist should compare results obtained from containers

(1) A and C
(2) B and C
(3) B and F
(4) C and D
(5) D and E

29. To compare the drainage properties of soil mixtures containing clay, the scientist should compare results obtained from containers

(1) A and D
(2) A and E
(3) B and D
(4) D and E
(5) D and F

30. Which of the following questions will the scientist be able to answer from the results of the experiment?

(1) Which soil mixture has the better drainage property: a mixture of sand and silt or a mixture of sand and clay?
(2) Which soil mixture would be the best in which to build an irrigation ditch from which there must be as little water seepage as possible?
(3) In which sample of soil would vegetables grow the best?
(4) Do different types of clay have different drainage properties?
(5) Which soil mixture would be best to use in a flower pot?

ANSWERS ARE ON PAGE 87.

31. The results of the experiment with the containers A, B, and C are shown by the graph below. Which of the following conclusions is best supported by information given in the passage and by the graph?

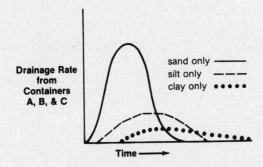

Drainage Rate from Containers A, B, & C

sand only ——————
silt only — — — —
clay only • • • • •

Time ⟶

(1) The smaller the soil particles, the better the drainage.
(2) The larger the soil particles, the better the drainage.
(3) Drainage is better when soil particles are tightly packed together.
(4) Clay drains more quickly than silt does.
(5) Not enough information is given to draw any conclusions about drainage.

Questions 32 and 33 are based on the following information.

Communications satellites are placed in synchronous orbits around the Earth. In a synchronous orbit, a satellite stays directly above a particular point on the Earth's surface at all times.

32. For a satellite to be in synchronous orbit, the satellite must make a complete trip around the Earth

(1) twice each day
(2) once each day
(3) twice each month
(4) once each month
(5) once each year

33. For which of the following activities would a synchronous-orbit satellite be useful?

A. photographing each of the continents

B. continually transmitting television programs from one country to another

C. measuring sunlight energy while staying in a position directly between the Earth and the sun

(1) A only
(2) B only
(3) C only
(4) A and B only
(5) A and C only

ANSWERS ARE ON PAGE 87.

Chemistry

Text pages
175–211

Questions 1–6 are based on the passage below.

Acid rain contains high levels of sulfuric acid and/or nitric acid. These acids form when sulfur dioxide and nitric oxide gases react chemically with oxygen and water in the atmosphere. Sulfur dioxide gas is produced when electric and industrial plants burn coal and oil fuels that contain sulfur. Nitric oxide is produced by car engines.

Acid rain can destroy fish and other water life, and it poses a threat to forests and croplands. It can also affect people, causing serious injury to the moist surfaces of the eyes and to the membranes in the lungs.

1. Two gaseous pollutants involved in the production of acid rain are
   (1) oxygen and water
   (2) coal and oil fuels
   (3) sulfuric acid and nitric acid
   (4) sulfur dioxide and nitric oxide
   (5) electric and industrial plants

2. Which of the activities listed below would contribute to acid rain?
   (1) boiling water on a stove
   (2) burning oil in a home furnace
   (3) popping a helium-filled balloon
   (4) using an electric current to break down water into oxygen and hydrogen gas
   (5) making a campfire with old branches and leaves

3. Acid rain can cause
   (1) nitric oxide emission from car engines
   (2) the reduction of gaseous pollutants from all sources
   (3) high levels of industrial waste
   (4) the formation of sulfuric acid in the atmosphere
   (5) the destruction of plant life

4. Each of the following could result directly in a decrease of acid rain in an industrial city *except*

   (1) an increase in the number of people walking or bicycling to work instead of driving
   (2) an increased use of sulfur-free coal by industries that use coal as a power source
   (3) an efficient and well-used public transportation system
   (4) an increase in public awareness about the dangers of being outside when acid rain is falling
   (5) an increased use of fuel-efficient cars by people who must drive to work

5. Which of the following is the *least* important "rule of thumb" for people living in a city that has a serious acid rain problem?

   (1) If possible, stay indoors when acid rain is falling.
   (2) Wear extra-warm clothes any time you must be outside when acid rain is falling.
   (3) Don't drive your car during the rainy season unless absolutely necessary.
   (4) If you get all wet in acid rain, take a shower and wash your clothes as soon as possible.
   (5) Wear a raincoat and use an umbrella if you must be outside when acid rain is falling.

6. Suppose a young boy walks home from school on a rainy day. His mother notices his eyes are red and takes him to the doctor. Which of the following is *not* information that the doctor would need to know in order to determine if the boy's eye condition is caused by acid rain?

   (1) whether the boy had been swimming that day in a pool
   (2) the chemical content of the rain falling that afternoon
   (3) whether the boy has a cold
   (4) whether the boy has any allergies
   (5) whether the boy is colorblind

ANSWERS ARE ON PAGE 87.

Questions 7–9 are based on the following information.

An advertisement for Rainbow Cleanser, a new sink and bathtub cleanser, states:

A. Rainbow Cleanser contains no phosphates.

B. Rainbow Cleanser is preferred in three out of four households where comparisons have been made.

C. The granules of Rainbow Cleanser are rainbow-colored.

D. No home is complete without Rainbow Cleanser.

7. In which of the above statements does the advertisement imply that Rainbow Cleanser has been tested by homemakers against other popular cleansers?

(1) A only
(2) B only
(3) C only
(4) D only
(5) A and D only

8. Which of the above statements is a fact that can be verified by a chemical analysis?

(1) A only
(2) B only
(3) C only
(4) D only
(5) A and B only

9. Phosphates are chemicals that stimulate the growth of algae in ponds and streams to such a degree that the water can become unsuitable for fish.
Statement A in the advertisement above might influence a potential buyer of Rainbow Cleanser who

(1) does not eat fish
(2) prefers laundry detergent that contains phosphates
(3) knows nothing about phosphates
(4) wants to buy the most effective cleanser on the market
(5) worries about the environmental impact of phosphates

Questions 10 and 11 refer to the following passage.

When chemical or physical reactions occur, energy is either given off or absorbed. In an exothermic reaction, energy is given off. An example is a forest fire, which produces heat and light energy. In an endothermic reaction, energy is absorbed. Photosynthesis—the absorption of sunlight by a plant in order to produce sugar—is an example.

10. Which of the following objects is undergoing an endothermic reaction?

(1) water turning into ice
(2) cookies baking in an oven
(3) a flashlight producing a beam of light
(4) a firecracker exploding
(5) a lit cigarette

11. If hydrogen (H) and oxygen (O) gases are allowed to freely mix, they explode when they chemically combine to form water (H_2O). From this information, you can deduce that when water is broken down into hydrogen and oxygen gases, the reaction that occurs is

(1) endothermic, because water has more chemical energy than separated hydrogen and oxygen gases
(2) endothermic, because water has less chemical energy than separated hydrogen and oxygen gases
(3) exothermic, because water has more chemical energy than separated hydrogen and oxygen gases
(4) exothermic, because water has less chemical energy than separated hydrogen and oxygen gases
(5) neither endothermic nor exothermic

ANSWERS ARE ON PAGE 88.

Questions 12–16 are based on the information below.

Viscosity is a measure of how much a fluid resists flowing and refers to the "thickness" of a liquid. Viscosity changes with temperature. For example, at room temperature the viscosity of syrup is much greater than the viscosity of water; the syrup pours more slowly than water. However, if syrup is heated, it pours almost as easily as water.

Viscosity is determined by the strength of chemical bonds that hold molecules of a liquid together. These bonds result in an internal resistance that retards the movement of molecules past one another. Heating causes molecules to move more quickly and weakens the bonds that hold them together.

12. At room temperature, which of the following liquids probably has the strongest molecular bonds?

    (1) orange juice
    (2) honey
    (3) milk
    (4) diet cola
    (5) water

13. From information given in the passage, you can conclude that one way of increasing the viscosity of a liquid is to

    (1) heat it until it's boiling
    (2) shake it until it's full of bubbles
    (3) cool it until it's frozen
    (4) dilute it with water
    (5) cool it but not freeze it

14. In winter, a car's engine is slower to turn over than in summer because the

    (1) electric current flows more slowly
    (2) gasoline flows more slowly
    (3) radiator water freezes
    (4) engine oil thickens
    (5) engine overheats

15. When sugar is added to water, both the viscosity and the boiling point increase. The boiling point is the temperature at which the liquid's molecules have enough energy to break the molecular bonds that hold them on the surface.

    A chemist would say that adding sugar causes the boiling point of water to increase because in a sugar/water solution the molecular bonds are

    (1) stronger than in pure water
    (2) the same as in pure water
    (3) weaker than in pure water
    (4) determined by the viscosity
    (5) more easily broken than in pure water

16. To which of the following people would viscosity have the *least* importance?

    (1) a speedboat designer
    (2) an automobile mechanic
    (3) a cook
    (4) a house painter
    (5) a lamp designer

ANSWERS ARE ON PAGE 88.

Questions 17–19 refer to the following information.

ELECTROLYSIS

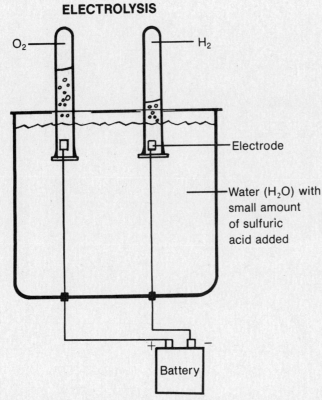

17. As a general chemistry term, *electrolysis* is best described as the use of

    (1) an electric current to cause bubbles to form in a liquid
    (2) a battery to cause an electric current to flow through a liquid
    (3) an electric current to break down a substance into its component molecules
    (4) a battery to create hydrogen and oxygen gases
    (5) water to create gas by causing electrodes to rust

18. You can infer from the drawing that the energy required to break down water into oxygen and hydrogen gases comes from

    (1) the inverted glass tubes
    (2) the heat energy of the water
    (3) heat energy found in the electrodes
    (4) the battery
    (5) the water molecules

19. Which of the following would speed up the rate at which oxygen and hydrogen gases are forming in the electrolysis experiment?

    (1) replacing the battery with one of higher voltage
    (2) replacing the battery with one of lower voltage
    (3) disconnecting the battery
    (4) increasing the amount of water in the jar
    (5) increasing the size of the inverted glass tubes

20. Ozone (O_3) is produced in the upper atmosphere when oxygen gas (O_2) absorbs high-energy sunlight. Remembering that the number of oxygen atoms must be the same on each side of the equation, which of the following equations correctly describes this reaction?

    (1) $O_2 + \text{energy} \longrightarrow O_3$
    (2) $O_2 + \text{energy} \longrightarrow 2O_3$
    (3) $2O_2 + \text{energy} \longrightarrow 3O_3$
    (4) $3O_2 + \text{energy} \longrightarrow 2O_3$
    (5) $3O_2 + \text{energy} \longrightarrow 3O_3$

21. Iron (Fe) can combine with oxygen (O) and produce any one of three different iron oxides: FeO, Fe_2O_3, and Fe_3O_4.

    Of the three oxides, FeO is the most unstable. If FeO is exposed to air, it forms Fe_2O_3. Which of the following equations correctly describes this reaction?

    (1) $FeO + O_2 \longrightarrow Fe_2O_3$
    (2) $FeO + O_2 \longrightarrow 2Fe_2O_3$
    (3) $2FeO + O_2 \longrightarrow Fe_2O_3$
    (4) $4FeO + O_2 \longrightarrow Fe_2O_3$
    (5) $4FeO + O_2 \longrightarrow 2Fe_2O_3$

ANSWERS ARE ON PAGE 88.

Questions 22–26 refer to the information below

loose molecular structure—A gas consists of atoms or molecules that rapidly move in straight lines until they collide with each other or with the walls of a container. The distances between these particles are very large compared to the size of the particles. In liquids and solids, the particles are much closer together.

temperature-dependent energy—Each atom or molecule of gas has kinetic energy (energy of motion) that increases as the temperature of the gas increases. As a gas becomes hotter, its molecules gain kinetic energy.

equal pressure—A gas exerts equal pressure (force per unit area) on each section of wall of any container to which it is confined.

diffusibility—When two gases are brought into contact, they will spontaneously mix—the molecules of each gas freely intermingle with the molecules of the other gas.

effusibility—Gas atoms or molecules will pass through a small opening from a container of higher pressure to a container of lower pressure.

22. A basketball keeps its round shape as more air is added. The fact that each part of the ball feels equally hard is related to

    (1) loose molecular structure
    (2) temperature-dependent energy
    (3) equal pressure
    (4) diffusibility
    (5) effusibility

23. A small child is holding a fully inflated balloon when suddenly she releases it. As air escapes through the mouth of the balloon, the balloon flies around the room. The balloon's motion is related to

    (1) loose molecular structure
    (2) temperature-dependent energy
    (3) equal pressure
    (4) diffusibility
    (5) effusibility

24. A gas cools when it uses its own kinetic energy to perform work. This happens in a *turbo* engine in which hot exhaust gas, before leaving the car, cools as it turns a small turbine on the engine. The turbine uses the energy of the exhaust gas to help increase the power of the engine.
    The cooling of exhaust gas in this way is an example of

    (1) loose molecular structure
    (2) temperature-dependent energy
    (3) equal pressure
    (4) diffusibility
    (5) effusibility

25. Unlike solids and liquids, gases can be compressed to a small fraction of their original volume. Fire extinguishers and other containers of compressed gas depend on this property. The reason that gases are so compressible is related to

    (1) loose molecular structure
    (2) temperature-dependent energy
    (3) equal pressure
    (4) diffusibility
    (5) effusibility

26. Just before leaving for work, Allison sprayed her hair lightly with perfume. Within a few seconds, the perfume's odor had spread throughout the room. In this instance, perfume vapor shows the property known as

    (1) loose molecular structure
    (2) temperature-dependent energy
    (3) equal pressure
    (4) diffusibility
    (5) effusibility

ANSWERS ARE ON PAGE 88.

Questions 27–29 are based on the information below.

The instructions on the back of a container of thinner for oil-based paint include the following warnings:

A. If swallowed, do not induce vomiting. Call poison control center, doctor, or hospital immediately.

B. Wash skin if contact occurs. Prolonged contact with skin can cause irritation.

C. In case of eye contact, immediately flush with water. If irritation persists, get medical attention.

27. You can conclude from warning A that the paint thinner

(1) has an awful taste that can cause you to vomit
(2) can give you a severe stomachache
(3) can seriously irritate or damage the membranes that line the throat and esophagus
(4) can quickly cause death if left in the stomach
(5) can irritate the walls of the small intestines to the point where they'll rupture

28. To protect public health and to avoid lawsuits, the manufacturers of the paint thinner use only chemicals that will not seriously injure skin upon contact. This precaution is based on the assumption that many people will

(1) accidentally spill paint thinner on themselves
(2) use their hands to mix paint thinner into paint
(3) use paint thinner to strip the varnish off of furniture
(4) refuse to use a dangerous product
(5) read the instructions on the paint thinner

29. When treating a person who has swallowed paint thinner, a doctor would need to know all of the following *except*

(1) the chemical content of the paint thinner swallowed
(2) the amount of paint thinner swallowed
(3) the time the paint thinner was swallowed
(4) the intended use of the paint thinner
(5) the types of liquids or foods most recently consumed

Questions 30 and 31 refer to the table below.

Composition of Several Types of Coal

	LIGNITE	SUBBITUMINOUS	BITUMINOUS	ANTHRACITE
Carbon, %	37	51	75	86
Hydrogen, %	7	6	5	3
Oxygen, %	48	35	9	4
Moisture, %	43	26	3	2
Nitrogen, %	0.7	1.0	1.5	0.9
Sulfur, %	0.6	0.3	0.9	0.6
Energy value, (kcal/kg)	3488	4784	7441	7683

30. The energy value of coal depends most on the content of

(1) carbon
(2) hydrogen
(3) oxygen
(4) nitrogen
(5) sulfur

31. The information presented on the table could help determine

(1) the abundance of each type of coal
(2) the region in which each type of coal is found
(3) the selling price of each type of coal
(4) the cost of digging each type of coal
(5) the estimated total reserves of all types of coal

ANSWERS ARE ON PAGE 89.

Questions 32 and 33 are based on the graph below.

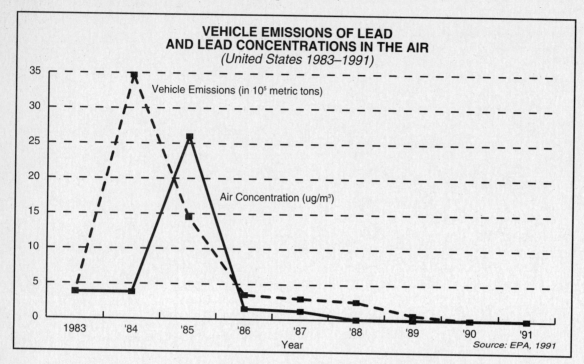

**VEHICLE EMISSIONS OF LEAD
AND LEAD CONCENTRATIONS IN THE AIR**
(United States 1983–1991)

Vehicle Emissions (in 10⁵ metric tons)

Air Concentration (ug/m³)

Year

Source: EPA, 1991

32. The best summary of the information in the graph above is that during the years 1983 to 1991,

(1) lead emissions decreased greatly
(2) lead pollution in the air decreased at about the same rate as vehicle emissions of lead
(3) the danger of lead poisoning in children decreased greatly
(4) new pollution-control devices were installed in automobiles
(5) lead pollution in the air decreased greatly

33. What additional information would you need to conclude that during the years 1983 to 1991 lead pollution in the air decreased mainly because of a decrease in lead emissions by vehicles?

A. whether lead used in gasoline results in lead pollution of the air

B. the number of people who switched from leaded to unleaded gasoline from 1983 to 1991

C. how total lead pollution from all other industries varied from 1983 to 1991

(1) A only   **(4)** A and C only
(2) B only   **(5)** B and C only
(3) C only

34. An emulsion is a suspension of small droplets of one liquid in a second liquid with which the first liquid will not mix freely. An example is the suspension of tiny droplets of milk fat in cream. Emulsions are common in food products and usually are typical of foods having a thick or creamy consistency.

Each of the following probably consists in part of at least one type of emulsion *except*

(1) mayonnaise
(2) a shaken bottle of oil and vinegar salad dressing
(3) spaghetti sauce
(4) apple cider
(5) yogurt

ANSWERS ARE ON PAGE 89.

Questions 35–38 are based on the following passage.

Acids, bases, and salts are chemicals that are part of our daily lives.

Organic acids are weak compounds that occur naturally. Citric acid has a sour taste and is found in lemons, grapefuits, and oranges. Acetic acid is found in vinegar and hydrochloric acid in the stomach's digestive juices.

Inorganic acids are strong, poisonous, and can cause severe skin burns. They are valuable in conducting electric currents and as industrial cleaners. For example, sulfuric acid is used in car batteries, while hydrochloric acid is used to clean metal surfaces.

Strong bases such as ammonia, liquid detergents, soap, and bleach are used as household cleansers. Weak base solutions are the main ingredient in antacids.

When a base is mixed with an acid, the two substances neutralize each other. The product is a salt (often a white crystalline powder) and water.

35. Based on the information in the passage, you can conclude that the cleaning agent in dishwashing liquid is probably

    (1) a strong base
    (2) a weak base
    (3) a strong acid
    (4) a weak acid
    (5) a salt

36. Lime can be used to neutralize acidic soil. From this information you can infer that lime is

    (1) an acid
    (2) a salt
    (3) an element
    (4) a base
    (5) a solvent

Questions 37 and 38 refer to the passage above and to the following additional information.

Chemists measure the strength of an acid or a base by use of pH values as shown below. A substance that has a pH of 7 is neutral; it is neither an acid nor a base.

pH VALUES OF COMMON SUBSTANCES

Battery acid	0.2	
Normal stomach acid	2.0	
Lemon juice	2.3	
Vinegar	2.8	
Soft drinks	3.0	
Apple juice	3.1	*more*
Orange juice	3.5	*acidic*
Banana	4.6	
Bread	5.5	
Potatoes	5.8	
Rainwater	6.2	
Milk	6.5	
Pure water	7.0	*neutral*
Eggs	7.8	
Hair shampoo	8.7	*more*
Milk of magnesia	10.6	*basic*
Household bleach	12.8	

37. Eaten together, which two substances are *least* likely to cause a change in the pH level of a person's stomach?

    (1) a piece of bread and an apple
    (2) a hard-boiled egg and a glass of milk
    (3) french fries and a coke
    (4) an orange and a glass of water
    (5) a banana and a glass of milk

38. Which of the following can you conclude from the information on the pH scale above?

    A. Vitamins obtained from some fruits are more acidic than vitamins obtained from dairy products.

    B. A mixture of lemon juice and orange juice is less acidic than normal stomach acid.

    C. Rainwater is more acidic than pure water due to the presence of automobile exhaust gases in the air.

    (1) A only   (4) A and B only
    (2) B only   (5) B and C only
    (3) C only

ANSWERS ARE ON PAGE 89.

Questions 39–42 refer to the following illustration.

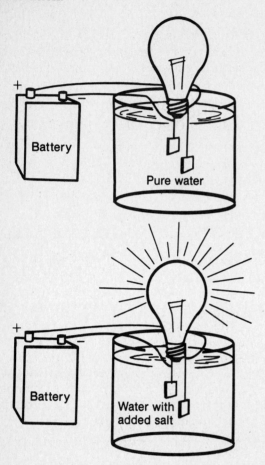

39. The key point made in the drawings above is that

(1) salt dissolves in pure water only when an electric current is flowing
(2) dissolved salt changes pure water into a conductor of electricity
(3) dissolved salt forms positive and negative ions in pure water
(4) dissolved salt changes pure water into a nonconductor of electricity
(5) electric appliances should never be placed in water

40. The equipment shown in the drawings could be used to test

(1) the strength of a certain battery
(2) the presence of salt in a sample of water
(3) the temperature of a sample of water
(4) the weight of a sample of water
(5) the wattage of a certain bulb

41. Which of the following liquids would have electrical properties similar to those of salt water?

(1) a water and antifreeze solution used in a car radiator
(2) distilled water used in a steam iron
(3) a water and sulfuric acid solution used in a car battery
(4) a water and sugar solution used in syrup
(5) a water and dye solution used to dye cloth

42. As shown by the graph below, the amount of current that a quart of water will conduct increases up to a certain point as more salt is added.

SOLUBILITY AND ELECTRIC CURRENT

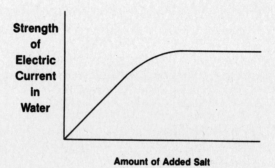

Which of the following statements is supported by information in the line graph?

A. Only a certain amount of salt will dissolve in a quart of water.

B. Because salt is heavier than water, salt that does not dissolve settles to the bottom of the container.

C. The strength of the electric current levels off after a certain amount of salt is added.

(1) A only
(2) B only
(3) C only
(4) A and B only
(5) A and C only

ANSWERS ARE ON PAGE 89.

Questions 43–47 refer to the passage below.

The boiling point of water depends on air pressure—the pressure on the surface of the water. The boiling point decreases as pressure is decreased and increases as the pressure is increased.

For example, at sea level, pure water boils at 212° F. But at an altitude of 3,500 feet above sea level, where the air pressure is much lower, the boiling point is only about 208° F. The boiling point of water at sea level rises above 212° F whenever the pressure on the water's surface is increased.

43. According to the passage, the boiling point of water is related to the

(1) surrounding air temperature
(2) outdoor air temperature
(3) air pressure on the water
(4) amount of water to be boiled
(5) amount of heat needed to boil the water

44. From information given in the passage, you can conclude that on top of Mount McKinley—at 20,320 feet above sea level—the boiling point of pure water is

(1) lower than 208° F
(2) 208° F
(3) between 208° F and 212° F
(4) 212° F
(5) greater than 212° F

45. Which of the following is true about living in the mountains compared to living along the sea shore?
In the mountains,

(1) the air pressure is higher
(2) frozen food thaws more quickly
(3) less energy is needed to cause water to boil
(4) the air temperature is higher
(5) the altitude is lower

46. A pressure cooker is an airtight container used for cooking certain foods. As water boils inside, the top of the pressure cooker prevents the evaporating water (steam) from escaping, thus increasing the pressure over the surface of the water.

In some situations, using a pressure cooker is more efficient than boiling water in an open pan. This is because water in a pressure cooker

(1) can be saved and reused
(2) can be brought to a boil with less heat energy
(3) can be brought to a boil more quickly
(4) boils at a higher temperature
(5) boils at a lower temperature

47. While vacationing in a mountain cabin, Gretta placed corn in boiling water and let it cook for 8 minutes. The next day at her coastal home, she again cooked corn using exactly the same method.

Compared to the corn cooked up in the mountains, the corn cooked at home

(1) was slightly more thoroughly cooked
(2) was slightly less thoroughly cooked
(3) tasted slightly less salty
(4) took slightly less time to cool
(5) took slightly more time to cool

ANSWERS ARE ON PAGE 89.

Physics

Questions 1–5 are based on the following passage and diagram.

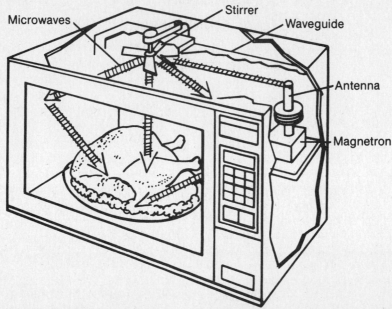

When a microwave oven is turned on, electricity flows through the power cord into a device called the magnetron. The magnetron changes electrical energy into microwave energy. The antenna sends microwaves down a hollow tube, called the waveguide, to the stirrer. The stirrer disperses the microwaves evenly around the oven's interior.

During cooking, the oven's walls reflect microwaves, which are absorbed only by water molecules in food. Because water is dispersed evenly in food, food placed in a microwave oven cooks evenly and quickly. This is unlike conventional ovens, which cook a food's outer layers first.

Another advantage is that the microwaves don't produce heat unless water molecules absorb them. This means that materials such as glass, paper, and most plastics can be safely used as cookware.

1. According to the passage, the function of a magnetron is to
   (1) disperse microwaves
   (2) produce electrical power
   (3) regulate cooking temperature
   (4) create a magnetic field
   (5) produce microwaves

2. Each of the following is an advantage of a microwave oven over a conventional oven *except*
   (1) the use of plastic cookware
   (2) more evenly cooked food
   (3) shorter cooking time
   (4) better-tasting food
   (5) less heat produced during cooking

3. If the stirrer in a microwave stopped working properly, the result would probably be
   (1) uncooked food
   (2) unevenly cooked food
   (3) frozen food
   (4) overcooked food
   (5) undercooked food

4. Which of the following correctly describes the path of the microwaves from the time they are created to the time they reach the oven's interior?
   (1) waveguide, stirrer, magnetron, antenna
   (2) stirrer, antenna, magnetron, waveguide
   (3) antenna, stirrer, magnetron, waveguide
   (4) magnetron, antenna, stirrer, waveguide
   (5) magnetron, antenna, waveguide, stirrer

50

ANSWERS ARE ON PAGE 90.

Questions 5–9 refer to the following passage.

Energy can appear in many forms and can change from one form to another. Six forms of energy are listed below.

electricity—energy carried by a moving stream of electrons

electromagnetic radiation—energy-carrying waves that can travel through a vacuum

sound—vibrations to which the ear is sensitive that travel through air or other substances

heat—the energy associated with the random motion of molecules

chemical energy—energy released when substances undergo chemical changes and new substances are formed

mechanical energy—energy associated with the movement of an everyday object like a baseball or a motorcycle

5. A liquid evaporates when fast-moving molecules on the liquid's surface break the bonds that hold them to the surface and escape into the air. The escaping molecules display the type of energy called

   (1) electricity
   (2) sound
   (3) heat
   (4) chemical energy
   (5) mechanical energy

6. A car's mileage is a measure of the car's efficiency of converting the chemical energy in gasoline to the form of energy known as

   (1) electricity
   (2) electromagnetic radiation
   (3) heat
   (4) chemical energy
   (5) mechanical energy

7. Sunlight, unlike other forms of energy, travels easily through the vacuum of space. The form of energy emitted by the sun is known as

   (1) electricity
   (2) electromagnetic radiation
   (3) sound
   (4) heat
   (5) chemical energy

8. In a car battery, electricity is created when lead at one electrode reacts with a solution of sulfuric acid and produces lead sulfate at a second electrode. A car battery makes practical use of

   (1) electromagnetic radiation
   (2) sound
   (3) heat
   (4) chemical energy
   (5) mechanical energy

9. In a superconductor, no energy is lost as electrons move from one point to another. Superconductors make use of

   (1) electricity
   (2) electromagnetic radiation
   (3) heat
   (4) sound
   (5) chemical energy

ANSWERS ARE ON PAGE 90.

Questions 10–13 refer to the information below.

OPERATION OF A HYDRAULIC JACK

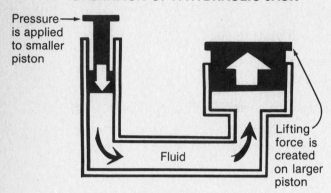

Pressure is applied to smaller piston

Fluid

Lifting force is created on larger piston

A hydraulic jack, shown above, consists of a cylinder and two pistons. When a force is applied to the smaller piston (shown on the left), that piston pushes down against the fluid. Pressure from the fluid creates an upward force on the larger piston. This upward force is in direct proportion to the area of the larger piston.

For example, suppose that the larger piston has twenty times the area of the smaller piston. A force of one pound pushing down on the smaller piston results in a twenty-pound force pushing up the larger piston. A five-pound force on the smaller piston results in a 100-pound lifting force on the larger piston.

When the larger piston of a hydraulic jack is placed under the corner of a car, a person can lift that corner by using a comparatively small amount of force on the smaller piston.

10. The key point made in the passage is that a hydraulic jack
    (1) uses more than one piston
    (2) enables you to raise a large piston by pushing down a small piston
    (3) creates a large lifting force from a much smaller pushing force
    (4) uses a fluid to transmit force from one piston to another
    (5) uses two different pistons

11. Suppose that in the hydraulic jack shown at left, the larger piston has an area that is 100 times that of the smaller one. What is the minimum force that must be applied to the smaller piston in order to create a lifting force at the larger piston that can support a 3,000 pound car?

    (1) 3 pounds
    (2) 30 pounds
    (3) 100 pounds
    (4) 300 pounds
    (5) 400 pounds

12. Some elevators that go up only a few floors use a type of hydraulic jack. When this type of elevator goes up,

    (1) the ropes in the elevator shaft lift the elevator
    (2) the smaller piston goes up
    (3) the larger piston goes up
    (4) the larger piston goes down
    (5) the elevator doors remain open

13. Pascal's law, which helps explain the operation of a hydraulic jack, states that a fluid in a container transmits pressure equally in all directions. Which of the following can be given as experimental proof of Pascal's law?

    A. The pressure inside an automobile tire increases as the tire's temperature increases.

    B. The pressure exerted on the outside lid of a bottle of cola is less than the pressure exerted on the inside of the lid.

    C. When the bottom of an open toothpaste tube is squeezed, toothpaste comes out of the top.

    (1) A only
    (2) B only
    (3) C only
    (4) A and B only
    (5) B and C only

ANSWERS ARE ON PAGE 90.

Question 14 refers to the following diagram.

MAIN COMPONENTS OF A COMPUTER

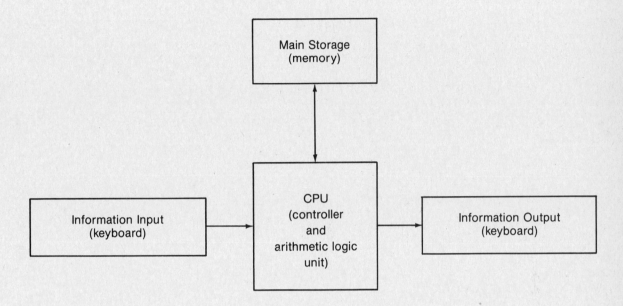

14. Looking at the diagram above, you can deduce that a CPU plays a role in a computer similar to the role played in the human body by the

    (1) heart
    (2) memory
    (3) nerves
    (4) brain
    (5) stomach

16. Luminous objects produce and give off visible light. Objects that only reflect light or that are lit up by electric power are not considered luminous. Which of the following is a luminous object?

    (1) a planet
    (2) a spaceship
    (3) the moon
    (4) a star
    (5) a man-made satellite

15. Which of the following observations is the best evidence that the creation of light is somehow related to the motion of electrons in matter?

    (1) Plants in a cave can carry on photosynthesis in the presence of an electric light.
    (2) Both light and free electrons can travel through the vacuum of space.
    (3) A light bulb glows when electric current flows through its filament.
    (4) Sunlight is composed of a spectrum of colors.
    (5) The heat created by an electric current can cause a match to light.

ANSWERS ARE ON PAGE 90.

Questions 17–19 refer to the following information.

During an evening storm, Maria is sitting in her living room reading. A floor lamp is on, and her radio is playing soft music. As the temperature slowly drops, Maria feels cold and plugs a space heater into a nearby wall socket. A few seconds after the space heater goes on, the lamp goes out but the radio keeps playing. Maria notices that the space heater has also gone off, even though the room is still very cold.

Maria then has the following thoughts.

A. "The bulb in the floor lamp is old and may have burned out."

B. "The radio is battery-powered."

C. "Lightning could have struck a nearby transformer and cut power to my house."

D. "I should try the kitchen lights and see if they work."

E. "The floor lamp and the heater are in the same electric circuit, and that circuit may be off."

17. Which of Maria's thoughts are hypotheses that suggest possible reasons why the floor lamp stopped working?

(1) A and B only
(2) A and C only
(3) B and D only
(4) A, C, and E only
(5) B, C, and D only

18. Suppose Maria discovers that the lights in the kitchen work. What is the most reasonable conclusion she can draw, knowing that the lamp and heater in the living room don't work?

(1) The kitchen lights and the living room wall sockets are not on the same electric circuit.
(2) Due to the storm, electrical service to her house has gone off.
(3) The bulb in the living room lamp is burned out.
(4) The space heater is broken.
(5) The kitchen lights use more electricity than the living room floor lamp.

19. Suppose Maria discovers that the lights in the kitchen don't work, and she concludes that lightning knocked out the power to her house. Which of the following would show that Maria is incorrect?

(1) Her neighbors' houses are completely dark.
(2) A voice on the radio says that the storm has knocked out power in only a few houses.
(3) Even though the electric stove works, none of the bedroom lights work.
(4) Her friend two blocks away calls and asks if Maria's power is also off.
(5) Maria has never before had trouble with electric circuits.

ANSWERS ARE ON PAGE 90.

Questions 20–23 refer to the diagram and passage below.

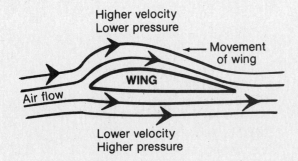

An airplane is much heavier than air. So how is it able to fly? The answer is related to Bernoulli's law, which states that air pressure decreases as air velocity increases.

The wings of most airplanes are curved on top and flat on bottom. Air that flows over the curved top of the wing moves faster than air flowing underneath, since it travels farther in the same amount of time. Correspondingly, air pressure is lower on the top of the wing and greater underneath. This pressure difference provides the lift that causes the plane to rise as it moves forward.

20. Each of the following is shaped to make use of Bernoulli's law *except*

(1) a boomerang
(2) an umbrella
(3) a frisbee
(4) a sail
(5) a seagull

21. The amount of lift an airplane will get from its wings depends on each of the following *except*

(1) the average width of each wing
(2) the length of each wing
(3) the curvature of the wing surfaces
(4) the weight of each wing
(5) the speed at which the plane is flying

22. Many airplanes have flaps attached to the plane's wing by hinges. Flaps are usually used during takeoff and landing. When the flaps are extended, the distance across the wing is increased. One purpose of the flaps is to

(1) turn the plane
(2) maintain the plane at normal altitude
(3) increase lift
(4) avoid turbulence
(5) avoid clouds

23. Which of the following graphs shows the correct relationship between pressure and velocity as described by Bernoulli's law?

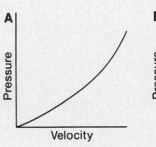
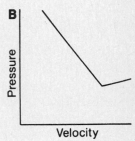

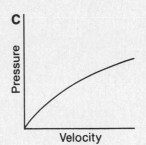
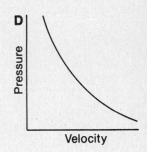

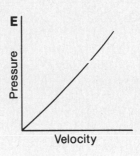

(1) A
(2) B
(3) C
(4) D
(5) E

ANSWERS ARE ON PAGE 90.

Questions 24–27 refer to the following information.

For an object to feel cool to the touch, heat must flow from your hand to the object. When heat leaves your skin, your skin feels cool, and this makes you aware that the object is cool.

Heat will flow from your hand only if the object you touch is at a lower temperature than your body temperature (about 98.6° F) and the object easily conducts heat. Room-temperature metal, for example, is a good conductor of heat and feels cool to the touch, while room-temperature cloth is a poor conductor and usually feels neither hot nor cold.

24. Which of the following best summarizes the passage above?

   (1) Hard objects tend to feel cooler to the touch than soft objects.
   (2) The sensation of coolness occurs when heat energy leaves your body.
   (3) An object that is at a lower temperature than 98.6° F cannot burn you.
   (4) Your hands are more sensitive to heat and cold than is the rest of your body.
   (5) Objects that are normally below 98.6° F tend to be good conductors of heat.

25. From information given in the passage, you can infer that

   (1) when metal and cloth touch, heat always flows from the metal to the cloth
   (2) any object at a temperature below 98.6° F feels cool to the touch
   (3) regardless of its temperature, a piece of metal always feels cool to the touch
   (4) a piece of metal that is at a temperature greater than 98.6° F will feel warm to the touch
   (5) any object at a temperature above 98.6° F feels warm to the touch

26. Which of the following would you expect to feel coolest to the touch?

   (1) an aluminum ruler at a room temperature of 84° F
   (2) a shirt at a room temperature of 65° F
   (3) an iron skillet at an outdoor temperature of 99° F
   (4) a glowing light bulb in a room where the air temperature is 58° F
   (5) a silver ring at a room temperature of 77° F

27. When you first pick up a metal spoon, it feels cool to the touch. Soon, however, the spoon feels neither warm nor cold. Which of the following best explains this observation?

   (1) Your hand gradually loses its ability to sense temperature.
   (2) Your hand gets cooler until it is the same temperature as the spoon.
   (3) The spoon gets warmer until it is the same temperature as your hand.
   (4) A sweat barrier stops the flow of heat from the spoon.
   (5) The spoon gradually loses its ability to conduct heat.

ANSWERS ARE ON PAGE 91.

Questions 28–30 refer to the information below.

As shown in the chart below, the loudness of sound is measured in units called *decibels*.

KIND OF SOUND	DECIBELS
Softest sound we can hear	0 — Hearing threshold
Normal breathing	10 — Barely audible
Rustling leaves	20
Soft whisper (15 ft)	30
Quiet office noise	50 — Quiet noise
Busy street traffic	70
Average factory noise	80
Heavy truck (45 ft.)	90 — Constant exposure endangers hearing
Subway train	100
Thunder	110
Rock concert with amplifiers	120 — Pain threshold
Jet taking off nearby	150

28. You can infer from the chart above that the decibel level of normal conversation is about

(1) 3
(2) 21
(3) 31
(4) 65
(5) 102

29. People prefer to have low decibel levels in each of the following *except*

(1) a church
(2) a recording studio
(3) a school
(4) an outdoor market
(5) a library

30. Which of the following statements is an opinion?

(1) Most people cannot understand what's said in a whisper of less than ten decibels.
(2) The sound of rustling leaves is more pleasant than the sound of a clock ticking.
(3) Loudness decreases as a person moves away from the source of sound.
(4) The decibel rating of a sound changes if the sound is made in water rather than in air.
(5) Repeated exposure to sounds above one hundred decibels can injure a person's hearing.

ANSWERS ARE ON PAGE 91.

Questions 31 and 32 are based on the table below.

AVERAGE COSTS OF OPERATING SELECTED CONSUMER PRODUCTS FOR 1 HOUR*	
Transistor radio	0.06¢
19-inch color TV	0.6¢
Electric typewriter	0.8¢
Power drill	1.5¢
Microwave oven	3.8¢
Clothes washer	8.3¢
Clothes iron	9.0¢
Hair dryer	9.3¢
Space heater	11.3¢
Range oven	30.0¢

* Based on an electric power cost of 7.5¢ per kilowatt-hour

31. The cost of operating an electric consumer product is most related to the

(1) weight of the product
(2) amount of space inside the product
(3) amount of noise made by the product
(4) amount of heat produced by the product
(5) size of the product

32. To conclude that the Gortner family spends more money for electricity watching television each month than they spend washing clothes, you would need to know the number of

A. days each month the TV is watched

B. hours each month the TV is watched

C. times each month the washing machine is on

D. hours each month the washing machine is used

(1) A and B only
(2) A and C only
(3) B and C only
(4) B and D only
(5) C and D only

ANSWERS ARE ON PAGE 91.

Practice Test

Directions: This science practice test will give you the opportunity to evaluate your readiness for the actual GED Science Test.

This test contains 66 questions. Some of the questions are based on short reading passages, and some of them require you to interpret a chart, graph, or diagram.

You should take approximately 95 minutes to complete this test. At the end of 95 minutes, stop and mark your place. Then finish the test. This will give you an idea of whether or not you can finish the real GED Test in the time allotted. Try to answer as many questions as you can. A blank will count as a wrong answer, so make a reasonable guess for questions you are not sure of.

When you are finished with the test, turn to the evaluation and scoring chart on page 81.

Questions 1 and 2 are based on the following passage and graph.

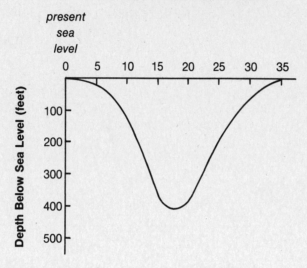

The Earth periodically experiences an ice age, a time of extreme cold when glaciers cover most of the land. As the Earth's temperature falls, glaciers get larger and ocean levels drop. Evaporating ocean water blows over the land and falls to Earth as freezing rain and snow. Since the atmosphere is so cold, little of the ice melts and returns to refill the oceans.

Recently, scientists have found evidence indicating that the average sea level has varied over the past 35,000 years as shown on the graph above.

1. For the time span covered by the graph, the sea level reached its lowest point

   (1) within the last 1,000 years
   (2) 10,000 years ago
   (3) 18,000 years ago
   (4) 26,000 years ago
   (5) more than 35,000 years ago

2. Which of the following conclusions is best supported by this graph?

   (1) The most recent ice age ended 18,000 years ago.
   (2) The most recent ice age began 20,000 years ago.
   (3) Sea level has stayed nearly constant over 35,000 years.
   (4) Scientists have been monitoring the sea level for 35,000 years.
   (5) Over the past 35,000 years, the sea level gradually rose and then gradually dropped.

ANSWERS ARE ON PAGE 79.

Questions 3–7 are based on the following article.

Used by nearly 15 million people in the United States, drugs to lower high blood pressure are a common factor in maintaining health. But, concerned over possible adverse effects, a number of researchers are exploring drugless methods to treat . . . [hypertension (high blood pressure), a condition that increases] . . . the risk of heart disease. . . .

[One] alternative may be that of control through nutrition. Researchers in Chicago and Minneapolis report the final results of a four-year study on the effects of overweight, excess salt and alcohol on blood pressure. They found that 39 percent of mild hypertensives who lost at least 10 pounds, decreased their sodium intake by 36 percent and drank no more than two alcoholic drinks per day maintained normal blood pressure without drugs, compared with only 5 percent of those who discontinued drug therapy but did not adjust their diet. However, initial blood pressure levels also affect the outcome.

—Excerpted from *Science Digest*

3. Which factor motivated researchers to investigate drugless therapy as a treatment for hypertension?

(1) a desire to find a way to control extremely high blood pressure
(2) a concern about the high cost of blood pressure medication
(3) an interest in seeing if diet affects overall health
(4) a concern about side effects of high blood pressure medication
(5) an interest in determining whether or not weight gain leads to hypertension

4. From information in the passage, you can conclude that

(1) thirty-nine percent of mild hypertensives are overweight
(2) excess salt and alcohol can lead to unwanted weight gain
(3) diet can play a role in reducing blood pressure
(4) weight loss is the most important factor in reducing blood pressure
(5) hypertensive patients should be under a doctor's supervision

5. In response to the study mentioned in the passage, many food manufacturers are likely to advertise

(1) low-salt canned foods
(2) alcoholic beverages
(3) bread made without preservatives
(4) cereals with a higher sugar content
(5) caffeine-free soft drinks

6. What is the best advice that doctors can give healthy patients who hope to avoid high blood pressure in the future?

A. Maintain weight within recommended limits.

B. Begin antihypertensive drug therapy.

C. Lose at least ten pounds.

D. Minimize salt and alcohol consumption.

(1) A and B only
(2) A and C only
(3) A and D only
(4) A, C, and D only
(5) A, B, C, and D

7. Which of the following studies would provide the best evidence in determining whether or not salt contributes to high blood pressure?

A study of two groups of mild hypertensives: one group that is put on a low-salt, 1500-calorie daily diet, and a second group that is put on a

(1) low-salt, 1000-calorie diet
(2) low-salt, 3000-calorie diet
(3) low-salt, 1500-calorie diet
(4) normal salt, 1500-calorie diet
(5) normal salt, 1000-calorie diet

ANSWERS ARE ON PAGE 79.

Question 8 refers to the illustration below.

PELVIC BONES

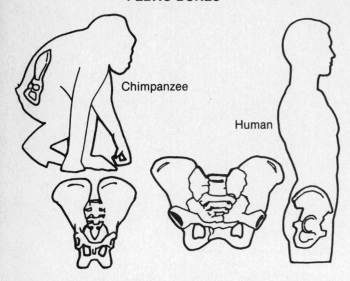

Chimpanzee

Human

8. The shape of pelvic bones in primates is related to the strength and function of upper leg muscles. Shown above are scale drawings of the pelvic bones of a human being and a chimpanzee. The shape of these hip bones is most likely related to the difference in the way that human beings and chimpanzees

   (1) swing by their arms
   (2) eat
   (3) walk upright
   (4) sleep
   (5) roll over

━━━━━━━━━━━

9. Carbon dioxide gas does not burn. For this reason, it is effective in putting out fires.

   Which additional fact(s) would enable you to conclude that a fire extinguisher containing carbon dioxide is an excellent household safety device?

   A. Water can cause an oil fire to spread and can increase the toxic fumes of an electrical fire.

   B. Carbon dioxide gas dissolves in water, forming a small amount of carbonic acid, which is useful as a preservative.

   C. Carbon dioxide gas is not harmful to humans.

   D. Pressurized carbon dioxide cools when it flows through the opening of its container and will quickly reduce the temperature of anything it touches.

   (1) A and C only
   (2) B and D only
   (3) C and D only
   (4) A, B, and C only
   (5) A, C, and D only

Questions 10 and 11 refer to the following passage.

The U.S. government has eliminated two-thirds of the soil erosion on the nation's most fragile farmland by paying farmers not to plow. Over 33 million acres of land are now enrolled in the Conservation Reserve Program (CRP). Participating farmers agree to retire their ground for ten years. In exchange the government pays a rental fee for five years and helps pay for establishing permanent land cover. This measure, part of the 1985 and 1990 farm bills, is hailed by the Department of Agriculture as "by far the best conservation program we've ever had."

—From *Science Digest*

10. According to the passage, an important cause of soil erosion in the United States is

    (1) real estate development of potential farmland
    (2) the failure of soil conservation programs
    (3) the plowing of erodible land by farmers
    (4) the high cost of price supports to farmers
    (5) off-road recreational vehicle use

11. When the Conservation Reserve Program is completed in 1999, the government may want to evaluate the program's success. Which of the following will be *most* relevant to this study?

    (1) the 1985 projected cost to taxpayers of the program
    (2) a comparison of the amount of soil erosion in 1985 with the amount in 1980
    (3) a comparison of the amount of available farmland in 1999 with the amount in 1985
    (4) a comparison of the amount of soil erosion in 1999 with the amount in 1985
    (5) a comparison of soil erosion in the United States with soil erosion in Canada

ANSWERS ARE ON PAGE 79.

Questions 12–14 are based on the passage and diagram below.

If you stir a spoonful of sugar into a glass of water, the sugar quickly dissolves and disappears. You know this if you've ever made fresh lemonade, coffee, or any other drink that contains water and sugar.

One entire cup of sugar will dissolve in one cup of water. If you try to dissolve more than one cup, sugar will settle on the bottom. When the water contains all the sugar it can hold, the solution is described as *saturated*.

12. The diagram above shows a solution of apple cider and sugar. Knowing that apple cider is mainly water, which of the following best explains why sugar is at the bottom of the glass?

(1) Sugar does not dissolve in apple cider.
(2) The sugar was placed in the glass before the apple cider was added.
(3) The apple cider was placed in the glass before the sugar was added.
(4) The apple cider in the glass is saturated with sugar.
(5) Sugar will dissolve in apple cider only when the cider is heated.

13. Which of the following experiments would enable you to determine for sure whether or not sugar dissolves in apple cider?

A. Add more sugar to the glass to see if the added sugar settles on the bottom.

B. Add unsweetened apple cider to the glass to see if the amount of sugar on the bottom decreases.

C. Pour half of the apple cider out of the glass to see if more sugar appears on the bottom.

(1) A only
(2) B only
(3) C only
(4) A and C only
(5) B and C only

14. If the cider is saturated with sugar, adding more sugar will change all of the following features *except* the

(1) amount of sugar on the bottom of the glass
(2) weight of the glass and its contents
(3) height of the cider in the glass
(4) total amount of sugar in the glass
(5) color of the cider

ANSWERS ARE ON PAGE 79.

Questions 15–18 are based on the following passage and graph.

By monitoring electrical impulses given off by the brain, scientists have discovered that people alternate between periods of light sleep and periods of deep sleep. The two sleep states seem to play different roles for the health of the body and the mind. During light sleep the body is restless and moves around on the bed; the mind is very active, and dreaming takes place. Because rapid eye movement takes place during light sleep (even though the eyelids are closed), light sleep is often referred to as REM sleep.

During deep sleep the body is much less active, and little, if any, dreaming occurs. Deep sleep is often referred to as non-REM sleep.

Infants alternate equally between these two sleep states. Adults, on the other hand, spend most of their time in the deep sleep state.

The typical sleep pattern of an adult is illustrated below.

**TYPICAL SLEEP PATTERN OF AN ADULT
HAVING A GOOD NIGHT'S SLEEP**
(assuming 8 hours of sleep)

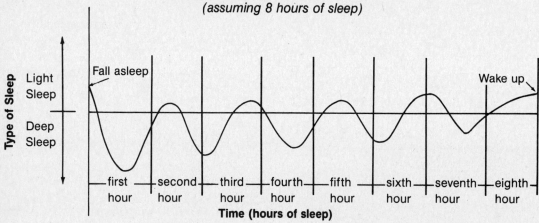

15. The passage mentions one difference between the way an infant sleeps and the way an adult sleeps. This difference is that, unlike an adult, an infant

  (1) cries often during sleep
  (2) gets hungrier while he or she sleeps
  (3) spends part of the time in deep sleep
  (4) spends half of the time in light sleep
  (5) wakes up often during sleep

16. From the graph above, you can see that during an average good night's sleep, an adult

  (1) spends an increasing amount of time in light sleep as the time asleep increases
  (2) spends an increasing amount of time in deep sleep as the time asleep increases
  (3) spends most of the first sleeping hour in light sleep
  (4) sleeps more deeply during the later hours of sleep than the earlier hours
  (5) wakes up during a deep sleep period

17. Which of the following is a conclusion you can draw based on the passage and graph?

  (1) An adult is more likely to remember a dream if he or she wakes up after four hours of sleep.
  (2) Adults spend more time sleeping than children do.
  (3) An adult who kicks off the covers during sleep spends more time in light sleep than in deep sleep.
  (4) Adults who sleep less than eight hours do not get enough sleep.
  (5) An adult does the most dreaming during the final hour of sleep.

ANSWERS ARE ON PAGE 79.

18. Which of the following additional facts supports the conclusion that infants dream more than adults dream during an average twenty-four-hour period?

A. Infants sleep more hours out of each twenty-four-hour period than adults sleep.

B. Infants often wake up and cry.

C. Infants cannot tell anyone else whether they dream or not.

D. During light sleep, infants show electrical brain patterns very similar to the patterns shown by adults when they are dreaming.

(1) A and B only
(2) A and D only
(3) B and C only
(4) B and D only
(5) D only

Questions 19 and 20 are based on the following passage.

The amount of gas that will dissolve in a liquid depends on two things: the pressure of that gas above the liquid surface and the temperature of the liquid. Increasing the pressure increases the amount of dissolved gas a liquid will hold; decreasing the pressure decreases the amount of dissolved gas.

Increasing the temperature, however, has the opposite effect: it *decreases* the amount of dissolved gas a liquid will hold. Decreasing the temperature *increases* the amount of dissolved gas.

19. When a bottle of a carbonated beverage like 7-Up is opened, it effervesces (bubbles) because carbon dioxide gas rapidly escapes from the liquid surface. The effervescence occurs because opening the bottle causes a

(1) rapid increase in temperature of the 7-Up
(2) slow increase in temperature of the 7-Up
(3) rapid decrease in temperature of the 7-Up
(4) rapid increase in pressure of carbon dioxide gas over the surface of the 7-Up
(5) rapid decrease in pressure of carbon dioxide gas over the surface of the 7-Up

20. Caps sometimes blow off the tops of ginger ale bottles when they are exposed to direct sunlight for a long time. This effect is most likely related to

(1) chemical changes that take place in sugar
(2) the weakening of the bottle caps
(3) a change in the temperature of the ginger ale
(4) a change in the color of the ginger ale
(5) the expansion of glass bottles

ANSWERS ARE ON PAGE 79.

Questions 21–25 are based on the following graph.

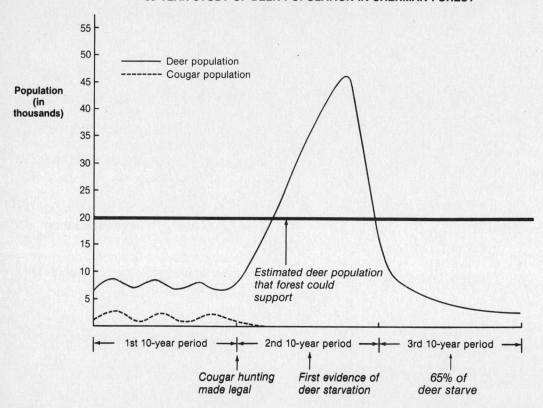

30-YEAR STUDY OF DEER POPULATION IN SHERMAN FOREST

21. After the decline of the cougar population in Sherman Forest, the deer population

  (1) increased continuously
  (2) increased to above its normal level for several years and then decreased to below its normal level
  (3) decreased to below its normal level for several years and then increased to above its normal level
  (4) decreased to its lowest level
  (5) reached its maximum stable level at 20,000 deer

22. You can infer from the graph that the rapid decline of the deer population was due to a(n)

  (1) inadequate water supply
  (2) lack of sufficient living space
  (3) inadequate food supply
  (4) increase in fatal diseases
  (5) increase in level of air pollution

23. Which of the following numbers on the graph is presented as an estimate rather than as a measurable quantity?

  (1) the deer population during the first ten years
  (2) the cougar population during the first ten years
  (3) the increase in the deer population that started at about the tenth year of the study
  (4) the maximum stable deer population of 20,000
  (5) the decrease in the deer population that started at about the seventeenth year of the study

ANSWERS ARE ON PAGE 79.

24. Of the following, which is the most practical and environmentally sound way to decrease the deer population of a forest?

   (1) Temporarily increase the length of the hunting season for female deer.
   (2) Destroy much of the foliage that deer use as food.
   (3) Separate all the male deer from the female deer.
   (4) Introduce new predators in the forest that kill deer.
   (5) Eliminate part of the deer's habitat by burning part of the forest.

25. A *predator* is an animal that kills and eats other animals (called *prey*). Cougars, for example, are predators, and deer are their prey. With these definitions in mind, which of the following generalizations is best supported by information given in the first ten-year segment of the graph?
   In a predator/prey relationship,

   (1) predators and prey search for food during different times of the day
   (2) predators and prey search for food during the same time of the day
   (3) an increase in the predator population always follows a decrease in the prey population
   (4) the predator population reaches its peak after the prey population reaches its peak
   (5) the predator population reaches its peak before the prey population reaches its peak

ANSWERS ARE ON PAGE 79.

Questions 26–30 refer to the following passage.

Many plants are adapted by nature so that their seeds are dispersed over a great distance. For some plants, the seeds are scattered when birds and other animals eat the fruit. Because they are protected by a coating that is not easily digested, swallowed seeds pass through an animal's digestive system unharmed. The seeds are taken wherever the animal goes.

Other types of plants produce fruit covered with sharp barbs that make the fruit inedible. In these plants, the barbs attach themselves to an animal's fur, and the animal disperses the seed by movement.

26. You can infer from the passage that the most important way an apple contributes to the growth of new apple trees is to

    (1) catch on the fur of passing animals
    (2) attract insects to pollinate the tree
    (3) provide nutritious food for wild animals
    (4) provide nutrients to the tree after it falls
    (5) attract animals that disperse apple seeds

27. By eating its fruit, wild animals can aid in the reproduction of the plant that produces each of the following fruits *except*

    (1) watermelons
    (2) tomatoes
    (3) seedless grapes
    (4) pears
    (5) blackberries

28. Which of the following factors is *most* related to the ability of an animal to disperse the seeds of a mulberry tree over a great distance?

    (1) the speed of the animal while running
    (2) the size of the animal
    (3) the types of predators that hunt the animal
    (4) whether the animal migrates in winter
    (5) whether the animal flies

29. Which of the following animals would be *most* effective in dispersing the seeds of plants that produce barbed fruit?

    (1) a wolf
    (2) a bluejay
    (3) a snake
    (4) an eagle
    (5) a frog

30. Which of the following additional adaptations would be *least* valuable to a plant that produces a barbed fruit that animals are unable to eat?

    (1) a strong smell that animals find attractive
    (2) an increase in the length of the barbs
    (3) an increase in the amount of fruit produced by the tree
    (4) a change in fruit taste, from bitter to sweet
    (5) an increase in the number of seeds found inside each fruit

ANSWERS ARE ON PAGE 79.

Questions *31–34* refer to the illustrations below.

**RATIO OF LAND
TO SEA**

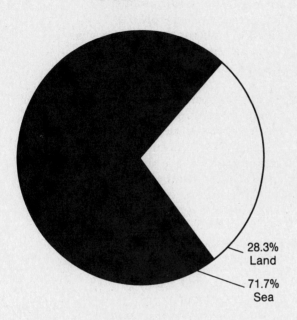

28.3%
Land

71.7%
Sea

**BREAKDOWN
OF LAND**

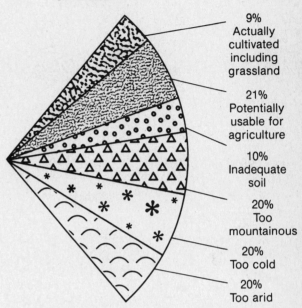

9%
Actually
cultivated
including
grassland

21%
Potentially
usable for
agriculture

10%
Inadequate
soil

20%
Too
mountainous

20%
Too cold

20%
Too arid

31. According to the illustrations, what total percent of land on Earth is either presently cultivated or potentially usable for agriculture?

(1) 9 percent
(2) 23 percent
(3) 30 percent
(4) 50 percent
(5) 64 percent

32. In which of the following categories would the continent Antarctica be placed?

(1) actually cultivated
(2) potentially usable for agriculture
(3) too mountainous
(4) too cold
(5) too arid

33. In which of the following categories would the corn fields of Nebraska be placed?

(1) actually cultivated
(2) potentially usable for agriculture
(3) too mountainous
(4) too cold
(5) too arid

34. One conclusion that can be drawn from the illustrations is that deserts (arid land) cover

(1) more of the Earth's surface than oceans
(2) less of the Earth's surface than cultivated land
(3) more of the Earth's surface than land that is too cold for cultivation
(4) about an equal amount of the Earth's surface as cultivated land
(5) about an equal amount of the Earth's surface as mountainous land

ANSWERS ARE ON PAGE 80.

Questions 35 and 36 are based on the drawing below.

DIFFERENCES IN THE PRODUCTION OF DRONE AND WORKER HONEYBEES

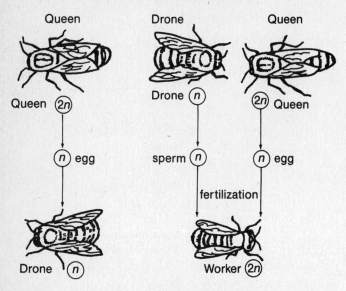

Relative chromosome number is indicated inside circles.

n = *number of chromosomes*

35. Which of the following best summarizes the information presented on the drawing above?

(1) Both the drone and worker honeybees develop from eggs laid by the queen.
(2) The queen is the most important type of honeybee in a hive.
(3) The worker honeybee is not capable of reproducing.
(4) Of the three types of honeybees in a hive, only the queen lays eggs.
(5) The worker honeybee develops from a fertilized egg while the drone develops from an unfertilized egg.

36. As a general rule, two animals can mate only if both have the same number of chromosomes. You can conclude from the drawing, though, that an exception to this rule is

A. the queen honeybee
B. the drone honeybee
C. the worker honeybee

(1) A only
(2) B only
(3) C only
(4) A and B only
(5) A and C only

37. A substance that is *biodegradable* is naturally decomposed by living things in the environment. Which of the following is biodegradable?

(1) a plastic milk container
(2) a rusting piece of iron
(3) a crumbling ancient rock wall
(4) a fallen dead tree
(5) an abandoned automobile tire

38. In any ecosystem, organisms compete for limited resources. Competition is most severe between members of the same species. However, it also occurs between organisms that are similar but not identical. For example, hole-nesting tree swallows compete with hole-nesting bluebirds for a limited number of nesting places.

Competition is *least* likely to occur between

(1) a whale and a dolphin
(2) two wolves
(3) a squirrel and a chipmunk
(4) a deer and a blackbird
(5) a sparrow and a robin

39. Penguins have wings, just as other birds do, but they use their wings for swimming only, not for flying. Penguins developed this specialized use of their wings through a process called *adaptive radiation*. In this process, an organism can develop a specialized use of a body structure that is unlike or is more specialized than the use that closely related organisms make of similar structures.

Which of the following is also an example of adaptive radiation?

(1) the gills of a trout
(2) the tail of a cow
(3) the antlers of a deer
(4) the neck of a giraffe
(5) the teeth of a lion

ANSWERS ARE ON PAGE 80.

Questions 40–43 refer to the following passage.

A controversial health issue today is the use of irradiation to preserve food. In this process, gamma rays are used to kill insects, parasites like trichina worms in pork, and bacteria like salmonella.

Food irradiation is used in over 35 countries now, but it has been slow to catch on in the United States. The FDA approved the process for harvested wheat and potatoes 30 years ago, but no other foods were approved for irradiation until the 1980s, when dried spices, slaughtered pork, fruits, and vegetables were added to the list. The nation's first food irradiation plant didn't open until 1992. In the years to come, however, concerns about food safety and convenience are expected to make food irradiation common here.

Although radiation is involved, irradiated food is not radioactive. It can be eaten immediately, or it can be vacuum-packed and stored safely for several years. Supporters of irradiation claim that it is a safe alternative to pesticides and preservatives.

However, critics point out that because irradiation can be used only on harvested food, pesticides will still be needed in the fields. What's more, they say that irradiation may kill odor-producing organisms that signal spoilage without killing the sources of food poisoning. Thus, irradiation may destroy an important natural warning system.

Critics also point out that irradiation changes the chemical makeup of food and creates carcinogens (cancer-causing chemicals). Supporters contend that an equal amount of carcinogens is produced when food is cooked or frozen.

40. Which of the following is the best summary of the passage above?

(1) Food irradiation is an accepted method of food preservation the world over.
(2) Although controversial, the use of food irradiation is increasing in the United States.
(3) Food irradiation does not result in deadly radioactive waste.
(4) Food irradiation can bring down the costs of dried foods.
(5) Because it produces high levels of carcinogens, food irradiation should not be allowed by the FDA.

41. When fruit is irradiated for a very long time, it turns squishy. One possible reason for this is that long exposure to gamma rays can

(1) break down a fruit's chromosomes
(2) alter the chemicals normally found in fruit
(3) break down a fruit's cell walls
(4) change the color and flavor of fruit
(5) destroy a fruit's cellular nuclei

42. If the FDA is considering whether to allow irradiation to be used for packaged meat, which information below is *least* relevant to their decision?

(1) the number of companies planning to use the irradiation process
(2) the types of carcinogens produced in the meat by the irradiation process
(3) the amount of radiation needed to kill the bacteria that would otherwise eventually spoil the meat
(4) the types of carcinogens naturally present in the meat
(5) the types of carcinogenic preservatives presently used in packaged meats

43. Which of the following facts is *least* important to FDA food scientists who are trying to determine what, if any, are the long-term dangers of food irradiation?

(1) The complete chemical makeup of any food is impossible to measure.
(2) So far, no adverse reactions to irradiation have been observed.
(3) Cancer associated with food irradiation may take twenty or more years to develop.
(4) The exact chemical changes caused by gamma radiation are impossible to determine.
(5) Because of accidents at nuclear power plants, many people fear the food irradiation process.

ANSWERS ARE ON PAGE 80.

Questions 44–49 refer to the information below.

Immunity is freedom from catching a certain disease. Five types of immunity are listed below.

inherited immunity—immunity that is inherited and may be permanent

naturally acquired active immunity—an often permanent immunity that occurs when a person's body naturally produces antibodies after being exposed to or infected by a disease

naturally acquired passive immunity—an immunity lasting for one year or less that occurs in a fetus or small infant because of antibodies passed to the offspring by the mother

artificially acquired active immunity—a long-term immunity that occurs when a person produces antibodies after being injected with a vaccine containing dead or weakened disease-causing organisms

artificially acquired passive immunity—usually a short-term immunity, lasting two weeks to several months, but may be a long-term immunity lasting years. Antibodies produced in an animal are injected into a person.

44. Some studies show that children who were breast-fed as babies are less likely to get certain diseases than children fed artificial baby formula. Doctors suspect that mother's milk provides antibodies that are not present in formula. If this is true, mother's milk provides

(1) inherited immunity
(2) naturally acquired active immunity
(3) naturally acquired passive immunity
(4) artificially acquired active immunity
(5) artificially acquired passive immunity

45. For protection against tetanus, an often fatal disease caused by bacteria, doctors recommend that children be given a tetanus shot at about two months of age. The antibodies present in a tetanus shot are produced by a horse! A tetanus shot creates

(1) inherited immunity
(2) naturally acquired active immunity
(3) naturally acquired passive immunity
(4) artificially acquired active immunity
(5) artificially acquired passive immunity

46. People contract chicken pox only once in their lives. After having chicken pox, a person is protected by a type of immunity known as

(1) inherited immunity
(2) naturally acquired active immunity
(3) naturally acquired passive immunity
(4) artificially acquired active immunity
(5) artificially acquired passive immunity

47. Although she has smoked two packs of cigarettes each day for the past forty years, Elvira, at age 68, shows no signs of lung cancer. Her mother also smoked heavily most of her life and lived to age 102. It seems possible that Elvira may be protected from lung cancer by a rare type of immunity called

(1) inherited immunity
(2) naturally acquired active immunity
(3) naturally acquired passive immunity
(4) artificially acquired active immunity
(5) artificially acquired passive immunity

48. In 1952 Dr. Jonas Salk developed the polio vaccine. This vaccine used weakened or inactivated viruses and succeeded in helping to nearly eliminate polio from developed countries. The immunity provided by Dr. Salk's vaccine is

(1) inherited immunity
(2) naturally acquired active immunity
(3) naturally acquired passive immunity
(4) artificially acquired active immunity
(5) artificially acquired passive immunity

ANSWERS ARE ON PAGE 80.

49. The line graph below shows how the natural concentration of antibodies in a person's bloodstream changes when the body is exposed at two different times to the same disease-causing organism. The primary immune response is often not sufficient to keep the person from getting the disease, whereas the secondary immune response may be.

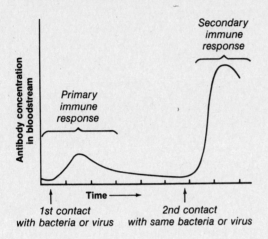

This graph is most related to the type of immunity classified as

(1) inherited immunity
(2) naturally acquired active immunity
(3) naturally acquired passive immunity
(4) artificially acquired active immunity
(5) artificially acquired passive immunity

—————————

50. Which of the following comments is an opinion?

(1) Whales communicate with one another by a series of cries.
(2) Dolphins and porpoises are actually two different types of toothed whales.
(3) Unless human values change worldwide, whale hunting will continue.
(4) A country's decision to allow whale hunting is not the concern of any other country.
(5) The largest animal alive on Earth today is the blue whale, weighing as much as 130 tons.

51. The Law of Conservation of Matter holds that matter is neither created nor destroyed during a chemical reaction. The number of atoms of each element must be the same on both sides of an equation that correctly represents a chemical reaction.

Applying the Law of Conservation of Matter, determine which of the following equations correctly represents the reaction that takes place when one molecule of propane gas, C_3H_8, combines with five molecules of oxygen (O_2) to create several molecules of carbon dioxide (CO_2) and water (H_2O).

(1) $C_3H_8 + 5O_2 \longrightarrow 3CO_2 + 2H_2O$
(2) $C_3H_8 + 5O_2 \longrightarrow 3CO_2 + 4H_2O$
(3) $C_3H_8 + 5O_2 \longrightarrow 4CO_2 + 2H_2O$
(4) $C_3H_8 + 5O_2 \longrightarrow 4CO_2 + 4H_2O$
(5) $C_3H_8 + 5O_2 \longrightarrow 4CO_2 + 5H_2O$

ANSWERS ARE ON PAGE 80.

Questions 52–55 are based on the following passage.

There's nothing surprising about using a battery to run a small motor. But imagine that battery is one that depends on bacteria to power it.

Such a device, one of the first to work well, was recently developed by Gerard Delaney and his colleagues at the Queen Elizabeth College in London. Called a biofuel cell, it is similar to a conventional battery in that it operates by converting chemical energy into electrical energy.

A conventional battery consists of an anode compartment and a cathode compartment that are joined by a wire. Chemical reactions in the anode generate electrons, which then move through the wire to the cathode. The flow of electrons is, in essence, electric current.

In a biofuel cell, however, the electrons are generated biochemically by bacteria living in the anode. They are produced as the microorganisms digest carbohydrates, such as sugars, that are fed to them. Normally, the bacteria use the electrons to fuel their own growth. But the British team discovered that if a chemical called thionine is placed in the compartment with them, it will steal the electrons away from the bacteria and transfer them to the anode's wire.

The inevitable result for the bacteria is death, and eventually new bacteria must be added to the battery to keep it running. But tests have shown that the microorganisms live for at least three months.

Wastes, such as those from food-processing factories and sewage plants, can be fed to the bacteria to generate power cheaply. And in remote parts of the world, where no reliable sources of electricity exist, the materials necessary to build a biofuel cell are available locally.

—From *Science Digest*

52. Which statement *best* summarizes the passage above?

(1) Batteries produce electric current by converting chemical energy into electrical energy.
(2) New bacteria must be added to a biofuel cell at three-month intervals.
(3) A biofuel cell makes it possible to use bacteria to produce electrical energy.
(4) A biofuel cell contains both an anode and a cathode.
(5) Biofuel cells may become the primary means of generating electricity in remote parts of the world.

53. Microorganisms are useful to human beings in many ways. Of the following, the *least* beneficial use that microorganisms serve is to

(1) break down human waste products in sewage treatment plants
(2) cause fermentation which turns a good wine into vinegar
(3) break down the remains of dead organisms in the soil
(4) cause fermentation which results in consumable alcohol
(5) act as a leavening agent in batters and doughs

54. Which of the following is *not* an advantage of a biofuel cell over a conventional battery?

(1) A biofuel cell is able to convert chemical energy to electrical energy.
(2) A biofuel cell generates inexpensive electrical power.
(3) A biofuel cell can be reused as more bacteria are added.
(4) The raw materials needed to make a biofuel cell are readily available worldwide.
(5) A biofuel cell increases the value of certain waste products.

55. If scientists forget to add thionine to a newly produced biofuel cell, which of the following will most likely result?

(1) The fuel cell will work for only about three months.
(2) The fuel cell will work, but its voltage will be reduced.
(3) The fuel cell will not work because the bacteria will all die.
(4) The fuel cell will not work because no moving electrons will be produced.
(5) The fuel cell will not work because the moving electrons will stop when they reach the cathode.

ANSWERS ARE ON PAGE 80.

Questions 56 and 57 are based on the information below.

The graphs below are called energy distribution charts. Each chart shows the average amount of light generated in each color band by the light source indicated: chart A represents natural outdoor light (sunlight on a clear day); chart B represents a typical fluorescent light.

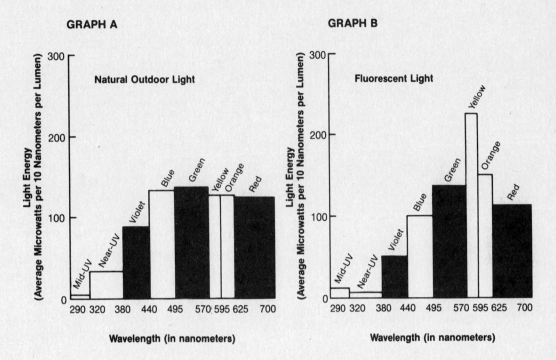

GRAPH A

GRAPH B

56. If a piece of paper appears bright white when viewed outside on a clear day, how would it appear when viewed in a room lit only by the fluorescent light represented by graph B?

   (1) bright white, the same as in outdoor light
   (2) slightly red
   (3) slightly blue
   (4) slightly yellow
   (5) slightly violet

57. Which two of the following are most likely to affect the energy distribution of sunlight that reaches your eyes?

   A. rain
   B. wind
   C. smog
   D. temperature

   (1) A and C
   (2) A and D
   (3) B and C
   (4) B and D
   (5) C and D

ANSWERS ARE ON PAGE 80.

Questions 58–60 refer to the following passage and illustration.

LIGHT ENTERING A HOLOGRAPHIC WINDOW

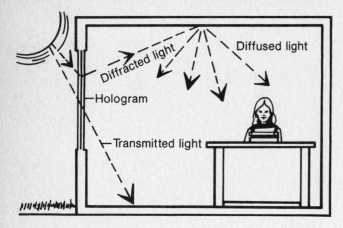

For many office dwellers, sunlight has become an all-too-scarce commodity. But now a hologram created by Photics, Inc., of Westford, Massachusetts, lets sunlight penetrate deep into buildings, thereby increasing ambience and reducing electricity bills.

To make the hologram, an interference pattern formed by two laser beams is imprinted on a photopolymer made by Polaroid. This film can then be stuck onto a window. The pattern diffracts incoming sun rays, bending them up and away from the window and creating a bright spot of light on the ceiling. Some light also comes through normally. The moving sun activates different regions of the hologram, allowing the illuminated ceiling area to remain the same, creating a constant light source. Costing $3 to $6 per square foot, the windows will pay for themselves in a year.

—From *Science Digest*

58. According to the passage, a hologram can be used to

  (1) increase the amount of sunlight passing through a window
  (2) decrease the amount of sunlight passing through a window
  (3) help keep a room warm in the wintertime
  (4) change the direction of sunlight passing through a window
  (5) store daytime light energy for nighttime use

59. A window hologram would most likely be used in a

  (1) bedroom
  (2) bathroom
  (3) hallway
  (4) closet
  (5) recreation room

60. The Athina Company is considering installing window holograms. They find out that each square foot of window hologram will cost them $3. What additional information would company officials need in order to determine whether they would save money by installing holograms?

A. the number and size of glass windows in the building

B. the number of new employees that Athina will hire in the future

C. the number of hours each day the company is open to the public

D. the amount that Athina presently spends for electric lights

  (1) A and B only
  (2) A and C only
  (3) A and D only
  (4) B and C only
  (5) B and D only

ANSWERS ARE ON PAGE 80.

Questions 61–63 refer to the passage below.

Many U.S. scientists hope that during the next few decades the United States will place a permanent colony on the moon. As a first step to possibly colonizing Mars and other planets, the moon colony would initially consist only of professional astronauts who would spend several months at a time on the lunar surface. Later, as the colony grew, other citizens could visit and perhaps even choose to reside permanently on the moon.

Reasons given in support of a moon colony include:

A. Gravitational effects are less on the moon than on the Earth.

B. The Soviet Union is ahead of the United States in space research and a moon colony is a way to regain worldwide prestige.

C. The moon has no atmosphere.

D. The thought of a moon colony is a fascinating idea that captures the interests of all peoples on Earth.

E. The moon is rich in minerals that have value on Earth.

61. Which of the above statements are opinions for which scientific evidence is not conclusive?

(1) A and B
(2) A and D
(3) B and D
(4) B and E
(5) D and E

62. Which of the above statements are facts related to advantages that the moon offers for certain types of scientific experiments?

(1) A and C
(2) B and C
(3) C and D
(4) A, B, and E
(5) B, D, and E

63. Which of the following best describes the attitude expressed in statement D?

(1) indifferent
(2) nonsupportive
(3) cautious
(4) excited
(5) uninformed

64. The ability of a living thing to maintain a stable set of conditions within its body is called *homeostasis.* An example of homeostasis is the capacity of warm-blooded animals to maintain a relatively constant body temperature.

When a warm-blooded animal becomes too hot, it sweats in order to cool off and maintain its normal temperature. This response is called a *homeostatic reflex.*

Which of the following responses would *not* be classified as a homeostatic reflex?

(1) an increase in heart rate during exercise
(2) shivering after jumping into a surprisingly cold lake
(3) gasping for air during a time of heavy air pollution
(4) jumping at the sound of an unexpected loud noise
(5) feeling hungry after awakening in the morning

ANSWERS ARE ON PAGE 80.

65. Oil flows at a different speed in each section of pipe shown below. According to the Principle of Continuity of Fluid Flow, the speed of the oil is greatest in the pipe with the smallest diameter and is least in the pipe with the largest diameter.

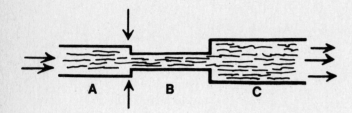

Which listing correctly identifies from slowest to fastest the relative speed of the oil flowing through the three sections of pipe?

(1) B, A, C
(2) B, C, A
(3) C, A, B
(4) C, B, A
(5) A, C, B

66. Energy can change from one form to another. A solar cell, for example, can change light energy into electrical energy. Which of the following devices is designed to change electrical energy into chemical energy?

(1) an electric fan
(2) a lightning rod
(3) an electric oven
(4) an electric light
(5) a battery charger

ANSWERS ARE ON PAGE 81.

Practice Test Answer Key

1. (3) The lowest point shown on the graph—about 400 feet below sea level—is between 15,000 years and 20,000 years.

2. (1) The sea level began to rise 18,000 years ago, as a result of melting glaciers, which ran off into the sea.

3. (4) According to the passage, researchers began to study drugless methods because of their concern over adverse effects of drugs.

4. (3) Thirty-nine percent of the people in the second study who changed their diet maintained normal blood pressure without drugs. Choice (4) is not true since reducing salt and alcohol intake is also important.

5. (1) The second study shows that eating too much salt may pose a health risk for people with high blood pressure. These people would be likely to buy low-salt products.

6. (3) These are reasonable guidelines based on the studies in the article. Healthy people should not begin drug therapy, and if they are already slim, they may not need to lose any weight at all, so B and C are wrong.

7. (4) For the study to be valid, there should be only one variable: the amount of salt. Both groups must consume the same number of calories.

8. (3) Since the shape of the pelvic bones is related to the function of the leg muscles, you can conclude that there is a similarity in the way human beings and chimpanzees walk upright.

9. (5) Fact A says that carbon dioxide can put out a fire in cases where water cannot. Fact C tells you that carbon dioxide is safe to use at home, and Fact D tells you that it is a good coolant. All are advantages of a fire extinguisher. Fact B is irrelevant.

10. (3) The passage cites the plowing of erodible land as a cause of soil erosion.

11. (4) The government will need to know the change in the amount of soil erosion during the period of the Conservation Reserve Program.

12. (4) If the apple cider-sugar solution is saturated, sugar will settle on the bottom of the glass. Choices (1) and (5) are false. Choices (2) and (3) are irrelevant.

13. (2) If the amount of sugar on the bottom of the glass decreases, the sugar is dissolving in the unsweetened apple cider. Neither A nor C will give you any useful information.

14. (5) Adding more sugar would not change the color of the cider, but it would change all of the other features listed.

15. (4) Infants alternate equally between the two sleep states.

16. (1) As time goes on, more and more of the curve goes above the line, in the light sleep area.

17. (5) An adult spends the most time in light sleep in the last hour, and dreaming only occurs during light sleep.

18. (2) Infants sleep more than adults do, so they must spend more time in light sleep. During light sleep, they show patterns similar to those shown by adults when they are dreaming.

19. (5) The cap maintains pressure on the carbon dioxide. When the cap is removed, the pressure is suddenly lowered.

20. (3) The heated ginger ale holds less dissolved carbon dioxide gas. This increases the pressure on the bottle cap.

21. (2) The line for deer (the thinner solid line) rises above the normal level at the beginning of the second ten-year period and dips below normal level again at the end of that period.

22. (3) Since the deer died of starvation, you can conclude that the problem was inadequate food supply.

23. (4) The maximum stable deer population cannot be counted since it is an ideal number. All of the other numbers could be arrived at by counting the deer or cougars in the forest.

24. (1) This is the only choice that, as an extension of an activity that's already taking place (hunting), would do no further damage to the environment. Choice (3) is impractical.

25. (4) Comparing the two wavy graph lines, you can see that each of the three peaks for the cougar (the predator) comes after a peak for deer (its prey).

26. (5) When animals eat the apples, seeds are dispersed. Choice (3) does not contribute to the tree population. None of the other choices are mentioned in the passage.

27. (3) Wild animals cannot help disperse the seeds of a fruit that has no seeds.

28. (5) An animal that flies could disperse the seeds over the greatest distance. None of the other choices is relevant.

29. **(1)** Of the animals listed, the wolf is the only one that has fur for barbed fruit to catch on.

30. **(4)** A change in fruit taste would not make any difference since animals cannot eat barbed fruit.

31. **(3)** Nine percent is actually cultivated and 21 percent is actually usable. 21 + 9 = 30

32. **(4)** Since almost all of Antarctica is covered with ice, the land there is too cold for cultivation.

33. **(1)** The corn fields are presently cultivated.

34. **(5)** According to the graph, 20 percent of the land is too arid for cultivation and 20 percent is too mountainous.

35. **(5)** The purpose of the diagram is to point out the differences in how worker bees and drones are produced.

36. **(4)** Since they mate with each other, both the queen and the drone are exceptions to this rule.

37. **(4)** A dead tree will be decomposed by bacteria and fungi. Choices (2), (3), and (5) may eventually be worn away by wind and water, which are nonliving.

38. **(4)** A deer and a blackbird are so dissimilar that, of the pairs listed, they would be competing the least for the same resources.

39. **(4)** The giraffe uses its neck to help reach for food. Other animals have necks but do not use them for this purpose.

40. **(2)** This sentence best combines all the ideas in the passage. Choice (1) is false. Choice (5) is suggested by the passage, but it is an opinion and represents only one side of the issue.

41. **(3)** Cell walls are what make fruits and vegetables firm. If a fruit's cell walls were broken down, it would become squishy.

42. **(1)** Before considering how many companies will use irradiation, the FDA must first make sure that the process is safe. The information in the other choices would help the FDA determine the safety of irradiation.

43. **(5)** Of the choices given, only choice (5), involving accidents at nuclear power plants, has no relationship to the danger of food irradiation.

44. **(3)** Antibodies are passed from the mother to the infant.

45. **(5)** The antibodies are produced in an animal and injected into a person.

46. **(2)** Permanent immunity resulting from exposure to a disease such as chicken pox is defined as naturally acquired active immunity.

47. **(1)** Immunity that seems to be passed on from mother to daughter is inherited immunity.

48. **(4)** A weakened virus (in this case, polio) is injected into a person, causing long-term immunity.

49. **(2)** When a person is exposed to a disease, antibodies are produced (shown as "primary immune response" on the graph). When the person is exposed to the disease a second time, the number of antibodies is much greater, so the person usually does not get the disease.

50. **(4)** This statement could not be proven or disproven. All of the other choices are facts.

51. **(2)** The reaction begins with three atoms of carbon, eight atoms of hydrogen, and ten atoms of oxygen. It ends with three atoms of carbon (3C), eight atoms of hydrogen ($4H_2$), and ten atoms of oxygen ($3O_2 + 4O$).

52. **(3)** Choice (3) covers all the ideas in the passage. Choices (1), (2), and (4) are true, but they are details.

53. **(2)** If microorganisms alter wine so that it spoils, they are not used beneficially.

54. **(1)** A battery can convert chemical energy also, so this is not an *advantage* of a biofuel cell.

55. **(4)** Thionine moves electrons from the anode to the wire leading to the cathode. Without thionine, there would be no moving electrons.

56. **(4)** In natural outdoor light, a piece of paper appears to be bright white because the amount of light energy generated by all colors is roughly the same. In fluorescent light, more yellow is generated than any other color, so the paper would appear yellow.

57. **(1)** Rain and smog absorb and scatter sunlight, so less of it reaches your eyes. Wind and temperature have no effect on how you perceive light.

58. **(4)** A hologram bends light rays up and away from the window.

59. **(5)** Of the rooms listed, the recreation room is the only one in which people would spend a lot of time during the day.

60. **(3)** Fact A will help determine how much light comes into the building. Fact D will help officials compare the cost of holograms with the cost of electric lights. Facts B and C are irrelevant.

61. **(3)** No one can prove that a moon colony would help the U.S. gain prestige or that a moon colony is fascinating.

62. (1) A place with less gravity than the Earth and no atmosphere would provide ideal conditions for certain experiments related to gravity and to astronomy.

63. (4) This person is clearly excited. The person feels that the idea of a moon colony is "fascinating" and that the peoples of other nations share this fascination.

64. (4) Jumping at a noise is just a reflex of the nervous system. Each of the others is related to the body's need to keep the heart beating, the lungs breathing, and to stay warm and well-fed.

65. (3) Oil flows slowest in the pipe with the largest diameter (C) and fastest in the pipe with the smallest diameter (B).

66. (5) A battery charger takes electrical energy from a wall socket and converts it into the chemical energy that powers the battery.

Practice Test Evaluation Chart

Check your answers using the answer key that starts on page 79. Then use the chart below to determine the skill and content areas you need to review. Circle any items that you got wrong and pay particular attention to areas where you missed half or more of the items. Review pages from *Contemporary's GED Test 3: Science* are indicated in *italic type*.

CONTENT AREA	SKILL AREA				
	Comprehension *pp. 17–31*	Application *pp. 33–41*	Analysis *pp. 43–61*	Evaluation *pp. 63–78*	Total Correct
Plant & Animal Biology *pp. 81–111*	21, **22**, 26, **35**	8, 27, 37, 38, 39	**23**, 24, 28, 30, **36**, 50	25, 29	_____/17
Human Biology *pp. 113–143*	3, 15, **16**	44, 45, 46, 47, 48, 49, 64	4, 5, **17**	6, 7, **18**	_____/16
Earth Science *pp. 145–173*	**1**, 10, **31**	**32**, **33**	**34**, 61	**2**, 11, 62, 63	_____/11
Chemistry *pp. 175–211*	52	51, 53	9, **12**, **14**, 19, 20, 54, 55	13	_____/11
Physics *pp. 213–251*	40, 58	**56**, 59, **65**, 66	41, **57**	42, 43, 60	_____/11
Total	_____/20	_____/20	_____/20	_____/13	_____/66

Note: Item numbers in **boldface type** are questions based on illustrations.

Answer Key

PLANT AND ANIMAL BIOLOGY
pages 3–14

Application

1. **(1)** The tundra is dry and cold. White animals, like the polar bear, live there.

2. **(3)** In the deciduous forest, trees' leaves change color in the fall.

3. **(4)** Grasslands provide rich grazing and farming land.

4. **(5)** The cholla is adapted to keep water loss to a minimum, so it must grow in a dry climate. Since it can withstand hot weather, it would not likely grow in the tundra.

5. **(2)** The cone-bearing trees in the coniferous forest often have needle-shaped leaves.

Analysis

6. **(2)** In order for the experimental results to be valid, conditions must be as equal as possible for each subject in the experiment. This means that the number of seeds planted must be equal as well as the amount of water given. However, Planter B must get four hours of sunshine a day while Planter C gets eight hours.

7. **(3)** The exact size of the planters would have little effect on plant growth. All of the other choices play important roles in plant growth.

Evaluation

8. **(2)** Both planters A and C get eight or more hours of sunshine a day, but each gets a different amount of water.

9. **(5)** Both planters C and D are watered once every two weeks, but each gets a different amount of sunshine.

10. **(2)** The experiment does not involve fertilizer.

11. **(5)** Warm water contains less dissolved oxygen, which trout need in order to breathe. Trout cannot live if they breathe only carbon dioxide, choice (1), or carbon monoxide, choice (3).

Application

12. **(4)** More trees can be planted when others are cut down, so forests are a renewable resource. There is no way to create any more of choices (1), (2), (3), or (5).

Comprehension

13. **(3)** The graph shows that chlorophyll absorbs about 90 percent of both blue and reddish orange light.

Application

14. **(3)** Since mushrooms are fungi, they have no chlorophyll. Therefore, they would have a different light-absorption graph. All the other choices represent green plants, which use chlorophyll to make food.

Analysis

15. **(2)** Green, the color of chlorophyll, lies between 500 and 600 on the horizontal axis.

16. **(3)** Animals raised in captivity have no predators in their environment. Choices (1), (2), (4), and (5) are not true.

17. **(3)** Each ring on the tree trunk represents a year of life. If you count the rings, you will find that there are 20.

18. **(2)** If there were no population-limiting factors, the trout population would continue to grow, as shown by the dotted curve. But since these factors do exist, the actual number of trout remains at about the same level over time.

19. **(1)** The actual number of trout is usually a bit more or less than the carrying capacity. If there are more trout than the lake can support, some of the trout die. If there are fewer, the actual number of trout increases.

Application

20. **(5)** Population-limiting factors cause a trout to die before the end of its natural lifespan. All of the other choices can curtail the lifespan of a trout.

Analysis

21. **(4)** If summer homes were built, residents would probably create water pollution. Then less of the lake would be habitable, so the number of trout that the lake can support—the carrying capacity—would go down.

82

Application

22. (5) A person's lungs always contain oxygen. Plants in a greenhouse are surrounded by air, which contains oxygen. The cheese also has air around it.

23. (4) There is no oxygen in an animal's digestive tract. Bacteria can survive there only if they can live without air.

Evaluation

24. (3) The biologist would need to know whether or not there was oxygen in the atmosphere. None of the other choices are relevant.

25. (1) Since the embryo is inside the yolk, and both are within the hard shell of the egg, the yolk gets smaller as the embryo grows.

Comprehension

26. (4) An organism needs both biotic and abiotic factors, so (2), (3), and (5) are wrong. However, some biotic and abiotic factors are harmful, so (1) is incorrect.

Application

27. (2) Bacteria are living things, not abiotic (nonliving). All of the other factors mentioned are nonliving.

28. (1) In a zoo, each animal is protected from the other animals and is fed regularly. This is not true in choices (2), (3), and (5).

Comprehension

29. (3) On the graph, the bars for both camel and horse end right after the line marked *8,000*. Choice (2) is wrong; the saber-toothed tiger was the *first* of the animals listed to become extinct. No information is given to support choices (1), (4), or (5).

Evaluation

30. (5) Extinction patterns in Europe would not affect animals in North America. All of the other choices would affect them.

Comprehension

31. (1) Look at the column labeled *Examples*. As you read down, you see that a kingdom has the most different kinds of organisms. Each category has progressively fewer kinds of organisms.

Application

32. (3) Look at the column labeled *Examples*. Both mammals and reptiles are included in the first three levels of classification, but the fourth and fifth levels include mammals only.

Comprehension

33. (4) This statement covers all of the ideas in the passage. Choice (2) is true, but it is only a detail. Choice (1) is not true according to the passage. While choice (5) could be true, it is not the main idea of the passage.

Analysis

34. (2) There is no way of interviewing birds to find out how they experience taste. Choices (1) and (4) can be observed, and choices (3) and (5) could be proven through chemical analysis.

35. (4) The robber fly's appearance helps it approach its food source, the bumblebee.

36. (3) Since the bola spider can trap prey using its bola, you can infer that the spider does not need a traditional web.

Comprehension

37. (3) Find Brand C in the column on the left-hand side. Then follow that row to your right until you reach the column labeled *22 oz.* That amount of Fertilizer C produced, on the average, a 15-inch plant. As you scan the rows that show average plant height, you see that 15 is the highest number on the table.

38. (3) Find the column labeled *20 oz.* and read downward. Choice (3) represents the correct order of plant height for that row, from tallest to shortest.

Evaluation

39. (3) As long as the plants are at least a few inches apart, it shouldn't matter how many feet apart they are. All of the other choices are necessary in order for the experiment to be valid.

40. (1) Each type of fertilizer produced the tallest plants when between 16 and 22 ounces of fertilizer were used. With more than 22 ounces of fertilizer, the plants were shorter.

41. (3) Whether something tastes good or bad is a matter of opinion. All of the other statements could be proven through experimentation.

HUMAN BIOLOGY
pages 15-29

Application

1. **(5)** Salmonella can develop in foods that are high in protein and moisture.

Analysis

2. **(2)** Food poisoning is most common during the summer months. July is the only summer month listed.

3. **(1)** Since cold air settles, the ice should be put in last so that the whole cooler will be cold. Then the coldest part of the cooler will be the bottom. The most perishable food—hamburger—should be put there.

4. **(4)** While it may be inconvenient, lack of a cooking area is not a health hazard. Salmonella can be found in fecal matter [choices (1) and (5)] and is carried by flies [choice (3)].

5. **(4)** Since buns are not moist or protein-rich, they do not need to be kept cool or cooked. Cleaning surfaces that people will eat from or cook on, as in choices (1) and (3), is always a good precaution.

Evaluation

6. **(5)** A product may not be safe to eat after its expiration date. Choice (3) may not help because some products, like canned goods, stay fresh for several years. Choices (1), (2), and (4) are irrelevant.

Comprehension

7. **(3)** Ultrasound, unlike x-rays, does not produce harmful radiation.

Application

8. **(3)** These injuries involve broken bones. The injuries named in B and C do not.

9. **(2)** Sound imaging does not work well in gases (like air). However, it can be used to check internal body organs, choices (3) and (5), or to find underwater objects, choices (1) and (4).

Analysis

10. **(2)** There is no way of proving how ultrasound may be used in the future.

~~rehension~~

~~ing~~ the adult skull to the newborn ~~you~~ can see that four distinct bones ~~and~~ a newborn's soft spot. On the ~~t,~~ these bones form a suture.

Application

12. **(1)** The protective skull bone has not yet grown together.

Comprehension

13. **(1)** Epilepsy is a disorder of nerve cells in the brain. An epileptic seizure is accompanied by a period of temporary unconsciousness.

14. **(3)** According to the third paragraph, epilepsy cannot be spread from one person to another.

Analysis

15. **(4)** A bus driver with this condition might lose control of the bus and crash.

Comprehension

16. **(4)** Vision is located in the occipital lobe, right above the brain stem.

17. **(2)** The diagram points out the different parts of the brain and their functions. Choices (4) and (5) are true, but they are details. Choices (1) and (3) cannot be determined from the information given.

Application

18. **(4)** This type of pain is not caused by an unhealthy activity but rather an event over which a person has no control.

Comprehension

19. **(5)** This statement covers all of the ideas in the passage. Choices (1), (2), and (3) are details. Choice (4) is not indicated in the passage.

20. **(3)** If tongue scraping had such bad effects, Alan Drinnan would not be scraping his tongue or telling others to do it.

Analysis

21. **(4)** The purpose of tongue scraping is to clean the tongue.

22. **(2)** Archaeologists have discovered tools that appear to be tongue scrapers. However, we can't prove how and why these tools were used. All of the other choices could be proven by experiments that can be carried out today.

Evaluation

23. **(1)** For the study to be valid, both groups of children must brush and floss so that those two conditions are the same for both groups. One group should scrape their tongues and the other should not.

Analysis

24. (3) The fact that ten different vitamins are listed suggests that the human body needs a variety of vitamins.

25. (4) No specific course of action is right for *all* children. Also, a statement about what someone should do is usually an opinion.

26. (5) Choice (5) discusses alcohol, but it does not relate alcohol to people's health.

Comprehension

27. (4) Enamel covers the outer part of the tooth.

28. (2) An average man's body is 44.8 percent muscle, while an average woman's body is 36 percent muscle. Likewise, a man's body is 14.1 percent bone, while a woman's is 12 percent bone.

Evaluation

29. (4) The average woman has a higher percent of total fat than the average man.

30. (2) Women's internal reproductive organs are larger than men's, so more fat is needed to protect them.

Comprehension

31. (1) Low body temperature is a symptom of heat exhaustion. The person should be kept warm until the body temperature returns to normal.

Application

32. (5) People who exercise need to drink plenty of water in order to avoid heat exhaustion (or heatstroke, if the people happen to be outside).

Analysis

33. (4) The passage says that the high temperature of heatstroke can cause brain damage and death.

Evaluation

34. (1) As long as the doctor knows more or less how old the woman is (middle-aged), her *exact* age is not important.

Comprehension

35. (2) On Graph A, find the point marked "at rest" on the vertical scale. This point is 0.3. Or, on Graph B, find 78 beats per minute on the graph line. Look directly to the left, and you will see 0.3 on the vertical scale.

36. (4) This statement best covers all of the ideas on Graph A. Choices (2) and (3) are details. Choices (1) and (5) could be inferred, but they are not the main idea.

Analysis

37. (3) First look at Graph A. After ten minutes, a person's heart is at the steady-state rate and the person is consuming 1.8 liters of oxygen per minute. Now find 1.8 on the vertical axis of Graph B. Look directly across from 1.8 until you see the graph line. That point on the line is above 140 beats per minute on the horizontal axis.

38. (1) A jogger consumes more oxygen than a person at rest, so a person jogging faster would consume even more oxygen. Since the jogger runs at a steady pace, he or she will have a steady-state level.

Comprehension

39. (3) In the left picture, the valve opens to let blood move through in one direction. When the direction of the blood reverses, as in the middle picture, the valve closes.

Analysis

40. (5) If less oxygen can enter the bloodstream with each breath, more blood would have to enter lung tissue in order to compensate.

Application

41. (5) This fact is not directly related to the question of whether leech saliva can help prevent cancer.

42. (3) Based on their observations, scientists think that blood clots are nests for tumor cells, but there is no proof.

43. (2) Gasic's experiment showed the cancer-fighting ability of leech saliva.

44. (1) To investigate keeping cancer from spreading, Gasic injected leech saliva into mice.

45. (4) A statement about how leech saliva will be used in the future is a prediction.

Comprehension

46. (3) Both the human jaw and the baboon jaw have sixteen teeth.

Application

47. (4) The large teeth in the front of the baboon's jaw are much better equipped to tear meat than the teeth in the human jaw. None of the other choices is related to the shape of the jaw.

Comprehension

48. (5) This statement covers all of the ideas in the passage. Choices (1), (2), and (4) are details.

49. (4) The cornea absorbs much of the ultraviolet light, or high-energy light, that strikes the eye.

Analysis

50. (5) All of the other activities require a person to spend a lot of time in bright sunlight, where the risk of retinal damage from blue light is the greatest.

Evaluation

51. (2) The purpose of sunglasses is to filter out rays that could harm the eye. The other choices are not related to health.

Comprehension

52. (5) The most effective method of birth control is the one for which the lowest percentage of women become pregnant while using it.

Analysis

53. (3) There is no way to prove that teenagers are acting sensibly and responsibly when they use birth control.

Evaluation

54. (1) Contraceptive foam, used by itself, is the least effective of the birth control methods listed. An advertisement for contraceptive foam would not highlight this fact.

EARTH SCIENCE
pages 30–39

Application

1. (4) Streak is the powdery color that a mineral leaves when rubbed against a hard surface such as a rock.

2. (3) Diamonds are useful because they are hard enough to cut almost any other material.

3. (1) Impurities like chromium, iron, and titanium affect the color of corundum.

4. (5) Cleavage refers to the way a mineral breaks or splits.

5. (2) Since silver and copper are metals, they both have a metallic luster.

6. (1) Fluorite can be scratched by glass, so it would not be hard enough to smooth the edges of a piece of glass.

Analysis

7. (4) Apatite, rated 5 on the scale, can be scratched by glass. Flurorite, rated 6, can scratch glass. Therefore, the rating of glass must be in between 5 and 6.

Evaluation

8. (4) The shapes of the moon and sun do not prove anything about the shape of the Earth.

Comprehension

9. (1) This is the best summary, since the passage explains why cloudy nights are warmer than clear nights. Choices (2) and (3) are true, but they are details.

Application

10. (4) There is little or no rainfall in a desert, and therefore, not much cloud cover. Since there are no clouds to trap the heat, the nighttime temperature would be lowest in the desert.

11. (3) A clear day would allow the most sunlight energy to reach the Earth. Total cloud cover at night would trap the most heat.

Analysis

12. (3) The two main substances in sea water, chlorine (55%) and sodium (31%), form when sodium chloride dissolves in water.

Comprehension

13. (3) Place something straight, like a pencil, along the graph line. Make sure that the end of the pencil extends as far as the horizontal axis. The point where the pencil crosses the dotted line (the freezing point) is directly above 8,000 feet.

Evaluation

14. (4) The mountain climber is the only one who needs to know about temperatures at various places on the mountain. Choice (1) works far above the mountaintops, and choice (2) works far below them.

Comprehension

15. (3) In both illustrations, there are breezes when cool air in one place moves toward warm air in another. If the air were the same temperature over land and sea, there would be no breeze.

Analysis

16. (5) If the air along the land got colder than the air over the water, the breeze could reverse its direction.

Comprehension

17. (4) The passage states that the spreading is caused by continual eruptions of underwater volcanoes.

Evaluation

18. (2) The continents move away from the ridge because the sea floor is spreading. Since the coastline on the left is as far from the ridge as the coastline on the right, the sea floor must be spreading at the same rate on both sides.

19. (1) A person who studies land climate does not have much use for information about the middle of the ocean floor.

Analysis

20. (1) According to the illustration, the North Star is directly above the North Pole.

21. (4) If the North Star were to move (for example, to the eastern part of the sky), it would be useless as a guide to direction.

Evaluation

22. (3) Since the dark side of the Earth points to a different place in winter, the sky looks different to us in winter.

Analysis

23. (4) The idea that comets left icy materials behind is a possible explanation for the presence of pieces of matter in space. A reasonable explanation of an observed fact is a hypothesis. Choices (1), (3), and (5) are facts; choice (2) is an opinion.

Comprehension

24. (3) The line on the graph dips to 60 degrees below zero at the point between the troposphere and the stratosphere.

25. (3) In the mesosphere, air temperature increases between 20 and 30 miles and begins to decrease over 30 miles.

Application

26. (2) Find 6 miles on the graph. This point is located in the troposphere, the layer closest to the ground. Throughout this layer, air temperature decreases as altitude increases.

Analysis

27. (4) For the experiment to be valid, all conditions must be kept the same except the type of soil tested. However, the weights of the soil types will probably differ, since each soil type is made up of a different combination of materials.

Evaluation

28. (2) B contains pure silt, and C contains pure sand.

29. (5) D and F are the only two soil mixtures with clay in them.

30. (2) From the experiment, the scientist could find out which soil drained the least water. That soil would be the best for the irrigation ditch.

31. (2) According to the passage, sand particles are larger than silt particles, which are larger than clay particles. According to the graph, sand drains best, silt second-best, and clay third.

32. (2) The Earth makes a complete 360-degree turn on its axis once each day. A satellite over a particular point on the Earth must also make the trip once a day.

Application

33. (2) A satellite that stays in a constant position between one country and another is suited to transmitting televised programs from one country to another. A synchronous orbit satellite would not be suitable for A or C because it stays over only one part of the Earth. It does not stay between the Earth and sun or pass over several continents.

CHEMISTRY
pages 40–49

Comprehension

1. (4) According to the passage, sulfur dioxide is a pollutant produced by industrial plants, and nitric oxide is a pollutant produced by car engines.

Application

2. (2) Oil contains sulfur. When oil is burned, sulfur dioxide is produced. The other choices produce gases that are not harmful to the environment.

Analysis

3. (5) Acid rain is known to destroy plant life. Choices (1) and (3) are causes of acid rain, not effects.

4. (4) Being more well-informed may help people protect themselves from acid rain, but it will not decrease the amount of acid rain.

Evaluation

5. **(2)** Whether or not you wear warm clothing in acid rain is irrelevant. All of the other choices either prevent contact with acid rain or minimize its ill effects [choice (4)].

6. **(5)** Colorblindness does not cause eye irritation. Each of the other choices indicates a possible source of eye irritation that must be considered if acid rain is to be ruled out.

Comprehension

7. **(2)** The statement implies that homemakers have compared Rainbow Cleanser with other cleansers.

Analysis

8. **(1)** A chemical analysis would show whether or not the cleanser contained phosphates.

9. **(5)** Since phosphates disrupt the environment of a pond or stream, a person concerned about the environment might be influenced by Statement A. Choices (1), (3), and (4) would not necessarily be concerned about the harmful effects of phosphates.

Application

10. **(2)** Cookies absorb heat as they bake, so they undergo an endothermic reaction. Each of the other choices gives off energy rather than absorbing it.

Analysis

11. **(2)** If an exothermic reaction occurs when hydrogen and oxygen gases combine to form water, then an endothermic reaction must occur when water is broken down into these same gases. If water gives off energy as it is created, then it must have less chemical energy than the separated oxygen and hydrogen gases.

Application

12. **(2)** Viscosity, or thickness, is determined by the strength of chemical bonds. Since honey is the thickest material listed, it would have the strongest chemical bonds.

Analysis

13. **(5)** Heating weakens the molecular bonds, so cooling would strengthen them. However, if the liquid were cooled until frozen (choice 3), it would no longer be a liquid.

14. **(4)** When the temperature is lower, viscosity increases. Choices (2) and (3) may also happen on a cold day, but these do not affect the engine.

15. **(1)** When sugar is added to water, the viscosity increases. Therefore, the strength of the molecular bonds must also increase.

Evaluation

16. **(5)** Viscosity would not be relevant to the design of a lamp. All of the other choices are people to whom the thickness of certain liquids is important.

Comprehension

17. **(3)** The diagram shows how electric current can be used to break a substance into its component molecules. Although water (hydrogen and oxygen) is used here, other compounds could be used.

18. **(4)** The energy to produce the electricity that flows through the wires must come from the battery.

Analysis

19. **(1)** If more electricity flowed through the water, the gases would form more quickly. Choices (2) and (3) would cause the gases to form more slowly, and choices (4) and (5) wouldn't make any difference.

Application

20. **(4)** On the left-hand side of the equation, there are three molecules of O_2, or six atoms of O (oxygen). On the right-hand side, there are two molecules of O_3, which is also six atoms of oxygen.

21. **(5)** The two molecules of Fe_2 on the right-hand side of the equation account for the four molecules of Fe on the left-hand side. The two molecules of O_3 account for the four atoms of oxygen in 4FeO and two atoms of oxygen in O_2.

22. **(3)** A gas, such as air, exerts equal pressure on each section of a wall of a container, such as a basketball.

23. **(5)** Air molecules pass from the high pressure of the balloon to the lower pressure of the surrounding air.

24. **(2)** As the amount of kinetic energy in the gas decreases, so does the temperature of the gas.

25. **(1)** Gases compress more easily than liquids or solids because there is so much more space between the particles. When a gas is compressed, the amount of space between particles is decreased.

26. (4) The molecules of perfume vapor freely mix with air molecules.

Analysis

27. (3) If the person were to vomit, the paint thinner would have to pass through the esophagus and throat a second time.

28. (1) People are likely to spill paint thinner on themselves. Choices (3) and (5) may happen, but they are not related to the protection of public health.

Evaluation

29. (4) The only relevant facts are those that deal with the person's consumption of the paint thinner. The foods most recently consumed are relevant since they may interact with the paint thinner.

Comprehension

30. (1) The energy value depends on the carbon content. Notice that lignite coal, which is 37% carbon, has an energy value of 3488, while anthracite coal, which is 86% carbon, has an energy value of 7683.

Evaluation

31. (3) Coal with a higher energy value would likely bring a higher selling price. The information on the table could not help you determine any of the other choices.

Comprehension

32. (2) To cover all the facts, a summary of this graph must include both the decline in lead pollution and the decline in vehicle emissions of lead.

Evaluation

33. (4) To draw this conclusion, you would need to know that other industries did not drastically lower their use of leaded fuels between 1983 and 1991.

Application

34. (4) Apple cider does not have a thick or creamy consistency.

35. (1) According to the passage, liquid detergents are strong bases.

36. (4) Since lime will make the soil less acidic, it is a base.

Analysis

37. (2) Milk, with a 6.5 pH, is slightly acidic. Eggs, with a 7.8 pH, are slightly basic. The acid and the base would tend to neutralize one another.

38. (2) Statement A cannot be concluded; the chart gives no information about vitamins. Statement B is true since lemon juice and orange juice both have lower pH ratings than stomach acid. You cannot conclude statement C, since the table gives no information about the source of acid in rainwater.

Comprehension

39. (2) The top light bulb is not lit, but the bottom one is. Salt has been added to the water in the bottom drawing. Therefore, pure water can conduct electricity only when salt is added to it.

Application

40. (2) The equipment could be used to test whether or not a sample of water had salt in it. If the sample were pure, the light would not go on; if it contained salt, the light would go on.

Evaluation

41. (3) The solution in the car battery conducts electricity, as salt water does.

42. (5) The line of the graph levels off after a certain amount of salt has been added. Therefore, after a certain point, no more salt will dissolve in a quart of water. The electric current can get stronger only when an increasing amount of salt is dissolving.

Comprehension

43. (3) The boiling point depends on the pressure on the surface of the water. None of the other choices has any effect on boiling point temperature.

Analysis

44. (1) The boiling point is 208° F at 3,500 feet above sea level. Since the peak of Mount McKinley is much higher, the boiling point temperature there would be lower than 208° F.

45. (3) Since the boiling point is lower at high altitudes, less energy is required to cause water to boil.

46. (4) When the pressure on the surface of the water is greater, the boiling point is higher.

47. (1) The corn cooked at home boils at a higher temperature than the corn cooked in the cabin. Since the same cooking time is used, the home-cooked corn is slightly more thoroughly cooked.

PHYSICS
pages 50–58
Comprehension

1. (5) The magnetron converts electrical energy into microwave energy.

2. (4) The passage does not say that food cooked in a microwave tastes better than food cooked in a regular oven. In any case, whether or not something tastes good is a matter of opinion.

Analysis

3. (2) The stirrer disperses microwaves evenly. If the stirrer stopped working, the food would be unevenly cooked.

4. (5) The magnetron generates microwaves. The antenna sends the microwaves down the waveguide to the stirrer.

Application

5. (3) Heat is associated with the motion of molecules, like the fast-moving molecules escaping the liquid surface.

6. (5) Mechanical energy is associated with the movement of an everyday object, like a car.

7. (2) Electromagnetic waves can travel through a vacuum.

8. (4) In a car battery, lead and sulfuric acid undergo changes, and lead sulfate is formed.

9. (1) Electricity is the motion of electrons.

Comprehension

10. (3) The purpose of a jack is to lift something heavy using a relatively small amount of force.

11. (2) The force on the smaller piston times the proportional difference in area equals the lifting force.
$$\text{force on smaller piston} \times 100 = 3{,}000$$
$$\text{force on smaller piston} = 3{,}000 \div 100$$
$$= 30$$

Application

12. (3) In a hydraulic jack, the larger piston provides the lifting force and therefore goes up.

Analysis

13. (3) When the bottom of a toothpaste tube is squeezed, the fluid (in this case, toothpaste) transmits pressure in all directions. Since the top of the tube is open, the toothpaste comes out of the top.

14. (4) The brain is similar to a computer's CPU in that it handles arithmetic and logic.

Evaluation

15. (3) When electrons flow through a light bulb filament, the light comes on. In choice (2), electrons travel through a vacuum, not through matter.

Application

16. (4) A star is the only object listed that gives off its own light. All of the other objects are visible to us on Earth because they reflect light from the sun.

Analysis

17. (4) The lamp may have stopped working because of a burned-out bulb, a broken circuit, or a power failure. Statements B and D are not related to the lamp.

18. (1) If the kitchen lights still work, then they are probably not on the same circuit as the appliances that don't work. Choice (2) is wrong, since the kitchen lights do, in fact, work.

Evaluation

19. (3) If the electric stove still works, then the house must still be receiving some electric power.

Application

20. (2) An umbrella, unlike the other objects, is not designed to fly.

Evaluation

21. (4) The weight of the wing is not related to the amount of pressure created by air flowing over the wing. If the wings are too heavy, the plane may not fly, but the amount of lift is the same.

Application

22. (3) When the distance across the wing is increased, the amount of lift produced by the wing increases, air pressure on top of the wing lessens and there is more surface that experiences lift.

Comprehension

23. (4) The horizontal axis shows velocity. Pressure is highest when velocity is lowest. As velocity increases, pressure decreases.

24. (2) This statement best covers all the ideas in the passage. None of the other choices are mentioned in the passage.

25. (4) Metal feels cool to the touch only when it is below 98.6° F. You can infer that, above that temperature, metal feels warm.

Application

26. (5) Metal feels cooler to the touch than cloth does. Of the metal objects listed, the ring is at the lowest temperature. A light bulb tends to be hot, regardless of room temperature.

Evaluation

27. (3) When an object feels cool to the touch, heat is flowing from your hand to the object. If it receives enough heat, the object will eventually be the same temperature as your hand.

Comprehension

28. (4) Normal conversation is slightly louder than quiet noise (50 decibels) but quieter than a subway train (100 decibels).

Analysis

29. (4) There is no need to control the noise level at an outdoor market.

30. (2) What is pleasant is a matter of opinion.

31. (4) The items that cost the most to operate— the oven, the space heater, and the hair dryer—are also those that generate the most heat.

Evaluation

32. (4) You need to know how much time was spent on both activities, but you don't need to know when the activities took place.